*MARY I*

*Queen Mary I* in the year of her marriage, 1554, by Hans Eworth.
(National Portrait Gallery, London)

# Mary I

## ROSALIND K MARSHALL

Published in association with
the National Portrait Gallery

London   HMSO

ISBN 0 11 290509 9

British Library Cataloguing in Publication Data
A CIP catalogue record for this book
is available from the British Library

Designed by HMSO

**HMSO publications are available from:**

**HMSO Publications Centre**
(Mail, fax and telephone orders only)
PO Box 276, London, SW8 5DT
Telephone orders 071-873 9090
General enquiries 071-873 0011
(queuing system in operation for both numbers)
Fax orders 071-873 8200

**HMSO Bookshops**
49 High Holborn, London, WC1V 6HB
(counter service only)
071-873 0011   Fax 071-873 8200
258 Broad Street, Birmingham, B1 2HE
021-643 3740   Fax 021-643 6510
33 Wine Street, Bristol, BS1 2BQ
0272-264306   Fax 0272-294515
9–21 Princess Street, Manchester, M60 8AS
061-834 7201   Fax 061-833 0634
16 Arthur Street, Belfast, BT1 4GD
0232-238451   Fax 0232-235401
71 Lothian Road, Edinburgh, EH3 9AZ
031-228 4181   Fax 031-229 2734

**HMSO's Accredited Agents**
(see Yellow Pages)

*and through good booksellers*

Printed in the United Kingdom for HMSO
Dd 294229   C40   7/93   3735

# CONTENTS

# AUTHOR'S NOTE

*S*PELLING and punctuation of quotations in both text and captions have been modernised, and French, Spanish, Latin and Italian have been translated into English. Dating is according to the Old Style Julian calendar in use in England throughout Mary's life.

*Henry VIII,* by an unknown artist, painted about 1520, when Mary was four.
(National Portrait Gallery, London)

# 1
## THE ONLY CHILD

O N 5 OCTOBER 1518 Princess Mary of England was taken to her mother's Presence Chamber in the Palace of Greenwich. A small, pretty child with reddish-gold hair and a pink and white complexion, she wore a new cloth-of-gold dress and a black velvet cap sewn with jewels. This was a very important occasion, her ladies had told her, and she must behave as a princess should. Mary was quick and intelligent, but she was really too young to understand. The women's words meant little to her. She knew only that she was being led into a high room where her father, King Henry VIII, stood in front of a throne, her mother, Catherine of Aragon, smiling at his side.

Obediently, Mary took up her position in front of the Queen, and waited quietly as a splendidly dressed gentleman made a long speech. When he had finished, another of her father's courtiers lifted her up in his arms and a stout figure in scarlet came to stand over her: Cardinal Wolsey, Lord Chancellor of England. Taking her small right hand in his, he slid a ring set with a huge diamond onto the tip of her finger, and then a foreign gentleman pushed it down over her knuckle. Two priests blessed her, everyone smiled approvingly, Cardinal Wolsey made a lengthy speech, and then he celebrated Mass. At two years old, Princess Mary was now betrothed to the Dauphin Francis, the French King's son and heir.

While she went back to her nursery with her ladies, the King, the Queen and all the courtiers feasted on fish and game, swans and larks, green ginger, gilt

*Catherine of Aragon*, by an unknown artist, painted about 1530, when Mary was fourteen. (National Portrait Gallery, London)

lozenges and sugared fruits. At the obligatory jousting afterwards, Henry's Tudor rose decorated the horses' accoutrements, entwined with Catherine's emblem, the pomegranate, and true-lovers'-knots linked the initials of the King and Queen.

Henry VIII, at twenty-seven, was not the alarming monster of his later years. Far from it. Over six feet tall, handsome, magnificently clad and with an expansive manner, he gloried in his own athletic prowess, loved music, lived in extravagant style and was devoted to his wife, Catherine of Aragon. Short, stout, pretty Catherine, with her smooth fair hair, her calm countenance and her dignified ways, suited him perfectly. Theirs had been an arranged marriage, of course. Her father was the ambitious, calculating King Ferdinand of Aragon, her mother, Isabella the Catholic, the energetic, intellectual Queen of Castile, famed throughout Christendom for having driven the Moors out of Spain. They made important, dynastic matches for all their children, and Catherine had first come to England to marry Henry's elder brother, Arthur, Prince of Wales.

When Arthur died a few months after the wedding, Catherine could have returned to her parents but she stayed on in England, anxious to preserve the Anglo-Spanish alliance. Arthur was gone now, but perhaps she could marry Henry instead. He was only ten, it was true, to her sixteen, but youth had never mattered in the business of arranging royal marriages. She waited and waited, for seven long years, while her father and King Henry VII of England wrangled over the terms. Sometimes she felt that they had forgotten her entirely, but she was stubborn and at last, in 1509, when the English King died, young Henry VIII made her his wife.

They were happy together. For all his ebullience there was an uncertainty about Henry, a hesitancy, perhaps the result of his over-protected childhood, shut away from other people by his anxious father. At any rate, he needed approval, and Catherine was always ready to reassure him, praise him, tell him that he truly was the ideal monarch. More mature than he in understanding as well as in years, she knew exactly how to handle him, and when she gave him advice she did so with such tact that he scarcely realised he was doing her bidding. He did not see a determined woman with a strong character; he saw only his properly humble, obedient wife.

In one respect only did she fail him in those early years. She did not give him a living child. Within months of their wedding there had been a still-born daughter and in 1511 a short-lived boy. There was probably another still-born son in 1513 and yet another, two years after that. It was an age of high infant mortality and such deaths were not unusual, but when the father was King of England, personal tragedy became political crisis. By 1516, people were saying openly that Catherine never would be able to have a healthy child.

When Mary was born, alive and well, at the Palace of Greenwich on 20 February 1516, Henry was triumphant. The baby might not be a boy, he told the Venetian ambassador who congratulated him and the Queen, but, 'We are both young. If it was a daughter this time, by the grace of God the son will follow.' Meanwhile, he was proud of this child of his, and he even allowed her the lavish christening he had planned for his prince.

On Wednesday of that same week, the baby was taken in procession to the Church of the Observant Friars, where Henry and Catherine had been married, seven years before. Lady Surrey had the honour of carrying the infant, the Dukes of Norfolk and Suffolk walking at either side, an ornate canopy borne over her head by four gentlemen, including the King's friend, Sir Thomas Boleyn. It was a short distance, for the church was near the palace gate, but the path was newly gravelled and strewn with fresh rushes, and the railings were hung with fine tapestries.

Inside, the church was ablaze with light and colour. The walls were draped with needlework hangings sewn with jewels and pearls, the silver royal font had been brought specially from Canterbury, and near it waited the dominating figure of Cardinal Wolsey, who would be the baby's godfather. Her godmothers were her great-aunt, Catherine, Countess of Devonshire, and the Duchess of Norfolk, a close friend of the Queen.

Mary was the name chosen for the new Princess, in honour of the Virgin, of course, but also for Henry's favourite sister, Mary, Duchess of Suffolk. She was solemnly christened and then she was confirmed, with another of Catherine's friends, the Countess of Salisbury, acting as godmother for that ceremony. There were fanfares, the choir sang, and afterwards there was feasting.

The celebrations complete, Henry lost no time in setting up the Princess's official household. More than fifty people were assigned to her service. Catherine Pole, already chosen for the important role of wet-nurse, must have been a relative of the Countess of Salisbury. Four women would rock the royal cradle, Margery Parker, Anne Bright, Ellen Hutton and Margery Cousin. Avice Wood was to be the Princess's personal laundress and there were chaplains, ladies and gentlewomen, pages and ushers. In charge of the household was the Lady Governess, Sir Thomas Bryan's reliable wife, Margaret.

For them, and indeed for the entire court, Mary was an admired and cosseted child, the centre of attention. The royal household was peripatetic, moving from one royal residence to the next as the year progressed, but in Mary's first months she and her parents spent an unusual amount of time at Greenwich and so she saw more of her parents than might have been expected. Moreover, in spite of Queen Catherine's subsequent pregnancies, Mary remained the King's only legitimate child, and her mother's cherished companion.

Her father was, of course, busy with affairs of state, but he remained charmed with her and he loved to show her off. A few days after her second birthday, Cardinal Wolsey escorted the Venetian ambassador to court. Henry at once had his daughter brought in, and the Cardinal bowed low over her hand. As the King's only child, she had precedence even over her own mother. Amongst the admiring throng was another Italian visitor, Friar Dionysius Memo, the organist of St Mark's, Venice. He was already staying at Henry's court and the little Princess had seen him before. Catching sight of him now, she amused her audience by shouting imperiously, 'Priest!' and gave him no peace until he sat down and played for her. Secure in her parents' love, she was a happy, confident and diverting child.

From her earliest days, ambassadors noted every detail of Mary's health and appearance, and ambitious courtiers plied her with gifts and sought to be associated with her. Cardinal Wolsey gave her a gold cup or some similar piece

Design by Hans Holbein for a brooch, probably for Mary. (Reproduced by courtesy of the Trustees of the British Museum)

3

*Henry VIII jousting before Catherine of Aragon* in 1511, to celebrate the birth of a short-lived son. (Great Tournament Roll of Westminster: College of Arms, London)

of gold plate each New Year's Day; other courtiers sent smocks, plate and little books; and her aunt, Mary, Duchess of Suffolk, was quick to enlist her as godmother for her own daughter, Frances, when the Princess was only eighteen months old. Mary did not attend the baptism in person, but Lady

*Cardinal Thomas Wolsey*, Mary's godfather, by an unknown artist. (National Portrait Gallery, London)

*Francis I of France*, Henry VIII's great rival, by Joos van Cleve. (The Duke of Buccleuch and Queensberry KT, Drumlanrig Castle, Dumfriesshire)

Elizabeth Grey stood proxy for her, while Lady Boleyn represented the Queen.

Keenly aware of the value of royal favour, the noblemen and their wives paid attention to the Princess as a way of remaining in her father's good graces, and they had an eye to the future, too. Even if Catherine of Aragon did succeed in giving Henry a son, her daughter would still be a significant pawn in the game of diplomacy, for she would no doubt be married off to some influential foreign prince. This thought was never far from Cardinal Wolsey's mind and, in February 1518, when he heard that the Queen of France had just presented her husband with a male heir, his response had been swift and to the point. 'The King of France has now got a son and His Majesty has a daughter,' he said. 'I will unite them by these means.' From then on he had not rested until the betrothal had been arranged.

At that time, an alliance with Francis I of France had seemed all-important, but as the months went by the situation altered. Another monarch appeared upon the scene to challenge Francis's dominance, and Mary's parents watched his progress with particular interest. He was Catherine's nephew, Charles, son of her sister, Joanna. His father had died when he was a small child, leaving his mother distracted with grief. He was from then onwards Duke of Burgundy. On the death of his grandfather, Ferdinand of Aragon, in 1516, he successfully claimed the crown of Spain, and in January 1519 he inherited vast territories in Germany and Eastern Europe from his grandfather, the Holy Roman Emperor, Maximilian I. That same summer he was elected Holy Roman Emperor. Francis I was furious, for he had wanted that title himself. It would be wise, Henry and Wolsey decided, to cultivate the friendship of this influential young man.

During the following summer they were able to see him for themselves, when Charles V paid a visit to England. At first the King and Queen were not

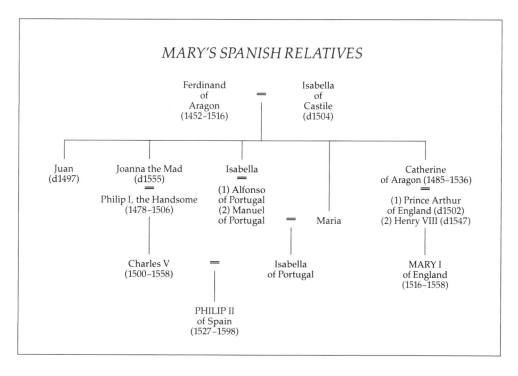

## MARY'S SPANISH RELATIVES

Ferdinand of Aragon (1452–1516) = Isabella of Castile (d1504)

Juan (d1497)

Joanna the Mad (d1555) = Philip I, the Handsome (1478–1506)

Isabella = (1) Alfonso of Portugal (2) Manuel of Portugal = Maria

Catherine of Aragon (1485–1536) = (1) Prince Arthur of England (d1502) (2) Henry VIII (d1547)

Charles V (1500–1558) = Isabella of Portugal

MARY I of England (1516–1558)

PHILIP II of Spain (1527–1598)

*Charles V* in about 1520,
a terracotta bust.
(Gruuthusemuseum, Bruges)

impressed. The new Emperor was an unprepossessing young man of twenty, with a lanky, gangling figure, bulbous eyes and the unfortunate Habsburg jaw, but he was courteous and pleasant, and they soon realised that he was highly intelligent. An alliance for mutual defence was agreed, but both sides looked for more than that. Henry VIII wanted to lay claim to the French Crown, and hoped that Charles would help him. For his part, the Emperor needed a wife. Who could be more suitable than his cousin, Princess Mary? She was only four, and she was the promised bride of the Dauphin, but these little difficulties need not stand in the way. Tentative approaches were made and, when Charles returned home, ambassadors and diplomats took up the negotiations. In August 1521, Henry and Charles signed the Treaty of Bruges. They would undertake a joint invasion of France and, when she was old enough, the Emperor would marry Mary.

They had met during his visit to England, of course, and now he took a close interest in her progress. Charles paid another visit to England himself in 1522, and that same year his emissaries to the English court were instructed to seek out the Princess and send back a report on her 'stature' and 'corpulence' as well as on her other qualities. When they finally met her, they were charmed to see that she was wearing 'on her bosom a golden brooch, ornamented with jewels forming the Emperor's name'. She had chosen Charles V, 'on St Valentine's Day for her valentine', so it seemed.

A fortnight later, the Queen promised them a special treat. The Princess would dance for them. As the leading ambassador put it, Mary 'did not have to be asked twice. She performed a slow dance and twirled so prettily that no woman in the world could do better'. After that, the Queen told her to show them a galliard, at which she acquitted herself 'marvellously well'. She then sat down at the spinet to play for them, displaying, they thought, 'unbelievable grace and skill, and such self-command as a woman of twenty might envy'. In short, they were greatly taken with her. 'She is pretty and very tall for her age, just turned seven,' they assured Charles, 'and a very fine young cousin indeed.'

By this time, Mary's education was proceeding apace. Queen Catherine was one of the most intellectual and best-educated ladies in England. Her own mother had seen to that. Isabella of Castile had herself taken lessons in Latin even as she led her armies against the Moors, and she employed the very best scholars of the day to educate not only her sons but her daughters. The result was that Erasmus, the leading humanist in all Christendom, described Catherine as a miracle of feminine learning, and it was she who had encouraged Henry VIII's much-vaunted interest in Renaissance studies.

She had gathered round her at the English court a circle of well-educated ladies and gentlemen, and when she began to worry about her daughter's education, her physician Dr Fernando Vittoria recommended his friend, Thomas Linacre, as a teacher. Linacre was particularly suited to the post, for he had once been Prince Arthur's tutor. Now, he drew up a plan of study for the Princess and the Latin textbook, *Rudimenta Grammatices,* which he devised for her, found great success in its day. When he died, not long after its publication, Catherine turned to the Spanish scholar, Juan Luis Vives, for further advice.

A graduate of the University of Paris, and a former student of Erasmus, Vives had been praised by Sir Thomas More as the best teacher in Europe. Catherine had already commissioned him to write a book on the education of women, and he had flatteringly based his recommendations on what he knew of her own upbringing. Young ladies of high birth, he said, should combine the feminine skills, such as spinning and needlework, with the intellectual pursuits of history, grammar, rhetoric and philosophy, and above all they must study religion. Girls were naturally more devout that boys, he believed, and so they would all the more readily appreciate the need for peace in Christendom, without which civilisation could never flourish.

Pacifism was, indeed, one of the main themes of his work, and from her later remarks it is evident that Mary studied his treatise well. Soon she was writing and speaking Latin and French and reading theology and history. When Vives' other commitments took him to the Low Countries, the Queen was only

*Queen Isabella of Castile*, Mary's Spanish grandmother, by an unknown artist. (In a private collection)

Thomas Linacre's *Rudimenta Grammatices*, 1524, dedicated to Mary. This was probably her own copy. (By permission of the British Library)

*Princess Mary*, aged about nine, wearing the brooch with the word 'Emperor' on it. This miniature is attributed to Lucas Horenbout.
(Brian Pilkington, Esq.)

*Juan Luis Vives*, Mary's tutor, engraved after a portrait attributed to Ribalta.
(Reproduced by courtesy of the Trustees of the British Museum)

LVDOVICVS VIVES, VALENTINVS.

*Splenduit in terra gelidam quæ reſpicit Arſton*
*Natum fœlici ſydus in Heſperia:*
*fllius ac totum radij effulſere per Orbem*
*Viues doſtrina & quos tulit & pietas.*

B 2

too pleased to supervise her daughter's studies, and she saw to it that Mary was carefully instructed in the Roman Catholic religion.

Catherine took her riding and hunting, too and, although she was spending an increasing amount of time away from her parents, they were always within easy reach. Her godmother, Lady Salisbury, seems to have taken over as Lady Governess, and there was a deep affection between them. Tall and dignified, the Countess was a widow in her fifties, but she had a family of her own and she knew how to speak to children. Special occasions were celebrated with amusing entertainments. The Christmas Mary had spent at Ditton Park when she was five had been enlivened by mummers and morris dancers. One of her valets had played the part of the Lord of Misrule in the traditional celebrations, and a decorated and gilded boar's head had formed the centrepiece at the banquet. When New Year's Eve came, she was back at her father's court, ready to enjoy the festivities.

Whenever he saw Mary, the King enquired eagerly about her musical accomplishments and by the summer of 1524, he was boasting to Charles V's latest ambassador, the Seigneur de Courrières, that the Princess played the spinet even better than he did himself, and was beginning to learn the lute.

The Seigneur was impressed, but Charles V's enthusiasm for his future bride was cooling rapidly. The Emperor's armies had been fighting the French in Italy and in February 1525 he scored a notable victory when his forces not only defeated Francis I at the Battle of Pavia, but managed to take him

8

prisoner. Henry VIII was delighted, imagining that Charles would now help him to seize the French Crown for himself.

Unfortunately for Henry, nothing was further from the Emperor's mind. His finances were exhausted, he had no desire to invade France and, in fact, in the aftermath of his Italian victory, he had little need of England as an ally. What he did require was a wife, and he could afford to wait no longer. He was twenty-five and it was time he had heirs. Mary of England was still only eight. Even if she was a mature child, she could not give him sons for another seven or eight years. A much more appropriate lady had attracted his attention, his Portuguese cousin, Princess Isabella. She was about his own age, and she was suitable in every way. That summer he broke off his engagement to Mary and married Isabella instead.

If Catherine of Aragon was disappointed, Henry VIII was deeply mortified by this sequence of events. Moreover, he had become increasingly worried by his wife's failure to provide him with a son. It seemed depressingly certain that his pretty daughter was going to be his only legitimate child. There had been no other pregnancies since Catherine's last still-birth in 1518. The Queen was obviously at the end of her childbearing years, and what was more, Henry had lost interest in her. The days when he had eagerly sought her approval were long past. Now she was a liability, a tiresome, domineering woman who no longer held any attraction for him.

Ever since the early years of their marriage he had taken a succession of mistresses, whom Catherine had politely ignored. His current lady friend, Sir Thomas Boleyn's daughter, Mary, had not given him any children, but a previous mistress had done so. Elizabeth Blount, one of Queen Catherine's own ladies, had borne him a son, known as Henry Fitzroy. He had no intention of reviving the affair with Bessie Blount, but would it not be better for England if he made her boy his heir instead of the Princess Mary? Everyone knew what chaos had resulted when medieval England was ruled by a female, Matilda. There would be no problem, it was true, if Mary were married to a man who could govern for her, but her latest fiancé had vanished and Henry was well aware that the Queen would never agree to their daughter marrying any close relative of Francis I of France, her dear nephew Charles V's greatest enemy.

Henry pondered the problem long and hard then suddenly, to his wife's dismay, he announced that he was making Elizabeth Blount's son, Henry Fitzroy, Duke of Richmond and Somerset, premier peer of England, Lord Admiral and a Knight of the Garter. For perhaps the first time in their lives, the Queen was bitterly angry with her husband. Hitherto, she had preserved a careful silence about his extra-marital activities, but this was different. It seemed to her and to many other people at court that the King had one aim in view. He meant to make the eight-year-old Duke his successor, instead of her beloved daughter, Mary. That was more than she could tolerate, and she told Henry so, in no uncertain terms.

He was furious, of course. He refused to listen to her, and soon afterwards he made another startling announcement. Mary was to go and live at Ludlow Castle. She was, after all, Princess of Wales. It was time that she took up her duties, and her presence on the Welsh border would facilitate the administration of justice in the principality. Catherine was appalled. He knew how devoted she was to their daughter. Was he separating them to punish her for her outspoken remarks about his bastard son? Some of her friends thought

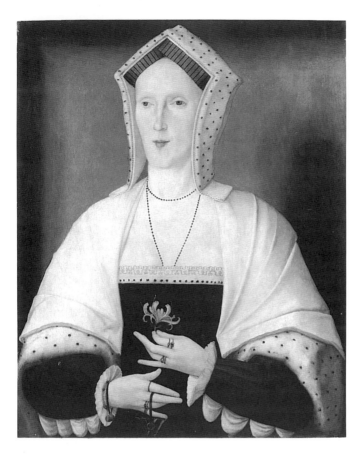

Possibly *Margaret Pole, Countess of Salisbury*, Mary's Lady Governess, by an unknown artist. (National Portrait Gallery, London)

not. They tried to comfort her by saying that Henry was strengthening Mary's position, drawing attention to the fact that whatever titles young Fitzroy might have, she remained Princess of Wales and therefore heir to his throne.

Henry's real motives remain a mystery, and the only certainty is that he did not appear to bear any malice towards Mary herself. Indeed, his arrangements for her welfare were full of fatherly concern. The Countess of Salisbury would be in charge of her household still, and that must have given the Queen some reassurance. Mary's other godmother Catherine, Countess of Devonshire, was to be one of the fifteen ladies who attended her. Her old nurse, Catherine Pole, would go along too, and so would Alice Baker, who had been one of her gentlewomen since her birth and Beatrice ap Rice, her laundress for the past six years.

Her household was being greatly augmented and – counting everyone from the steward and chamberlain to the yeomen and grooms, from the physician and apothecary to the valets and cooks, from the great lords of the Council of Wales to their personal servants – she would have three hundred and four people with her, surely the retinue of the heir to the throne.

They all set out for the west in August 1525, travelling first to Thornbury Castle, near Bristol, a pleasant mansion formerly owned by the Dukes of Buckingham. After some weeks there, they moved to Ludlow Castle, a formidable Norman stronghold built on a steep rock overlooking the River

Teme. This would be the Princess's principal residence, and she must have viewed it with considerable interest for it was there that Catherine of Aragon had passed her brief married life with Prince Arthur. When Ludlow had to be vacated so that it could be cleaned, Mary travelled to Tickenhill in Shropshire and Hartlebury in Worcestershire.

Wherever she went, Lady Salisbury had strict instructions from the King that his daughter's rooms were to be kept 'pure, sweet, clean and wholesome'. Her clothes must be properly laundered, and her food had to be 'pure, well-prepared, dressed and served with comfortable, joyous and merry communication'. Her tutor, Mr Richard Fetherstone, a renowned Cambridge scholar, would supervise her lessons, and she was to play upon the virginals and other instruments, although never to the extent that she became fatigued. In between lessons, she was to be sure to take gentle exercise, walking in the gardens for the sake of her 'health, solace and comfort', and she should dance from time to time, too.

The Queen missed her daughter sadly when she had gone, not least because the King was spending more and more time apart from her. She was delighted when Mary wrote to her from Ludlow, and in reply she asked wistfully about the Princess's progress in Latin. While declaring bravely, 'I am glad that you shall change from me to Master Fetherstone, for that shall do you much good to learn by him to write aright,' she could not help remembering sadly the hours she had spent helping Mary herself. Perhaps she might be allowed to see her daughter's exercises, once her tutor had looked at them, of course? 'It shall be a great comfort to me to see you keep your Latin and fair writing and all,' she explained. Encouraged by her mother's close interest, Mary toiled diligently at her books and, when she was eleven, she so much impressed the cultivated Lord Morley with a translation into English of a prayer by Thomas Aquinas, that he passed it on to his wife and daughters and even mentioned it in one of his own learned publications.

Plans for Mary to return to court for Christmas 1525 had come to nothing, and more than eighteen months were to pass before she saw her parents again. Not until the spring of 1527 did she receive word that she was to travel to Greenwich Palace. Once more, her future was to be discussed. King Francis I had the previous year been released from his imprisonment in Spain, and now he sent messengers to London suggesting that either he or his second son Henry, Duke of Orleans, should marry Princess Mary. Francis was only two years younger than Henry VIII, and his son was a hostage in Spain. These were minor considerations, however, for Henry had decided that the time had come to sign a treaty of friendship with France.

Mary was eleven now, but she looked a good deal younger. Indeed, when the French ambassadors saw her, they were dismayed. She was, they reported, 'so thin, spare and small as to make it impossible to be married for the next three years'. Legally she would be old enough to become a wife as soon as she was twelve, but she was far too immature physically to be a bride. Worrying though this was, it did not hinder the negotiations. The treaty of friendship between France and England was duly signed on 30 April, leaving it undecided whether Francis or his son should be the eventual bridegroom, and on 5 May the French ambassadors attended a magnificent banquet to celebrate.

Henry had given orders for a temporary banqueting hall and theatre to be constructed at Greenwich for the occasion, and supper was served in the hall,

Thornbury Castle, near Bristol, where Mary stayed on her way to Ludlow.
(Photograph courtesy of Thornbury Castle Hotel)

Ludlow Castle, Shropshire.
(Photograph, Gerald D'Urban)

Treaty for the marriage of eleven-year-old Mary to the eight-year-old Duke of Orleans, 18 August 1527.
(Public Record Office, E30/1112 [*LP* IV ii, 3356/7])

beneath a sumptuous red brocade ceiling decorated with Tudor roses and Catherine's pomegranates. The walls were hung with rich tapestries, and an impressive array of gold plate was displayed on a huge dresser. Musicians and minstrels entertained the company throughout the meal and, when it was over, the King led the way through a triumphal arch to the theatre. Suitably impressed by the lavish decorations, the French contingent turned round at once when he commanded them to look at the other side of the arch. There, before them, was a lively painting of the occasion some years earlier, when Henry and his army had successfully besieged and taken the French town of Thérouanne.

Laughing at their discomfiture, he limped across the fleur-de-lis-encrusted carpet to the tiers of seats at each side. He had recently hurt his foot, and it was not quite better yet. Indicating that his guests must sit in the front row so that they would have a good view of the masque which followed, he took his place on the royal throne on a dais facing the stage. The entertainment began with eight minstrels who appeared, singing English songs. In the midst was Mercury, a young boy in a blue silk gown embroidered with gold. The music over, Mercury made a solemn speech in Latin, praising the great friendship between England and France, and then there was a lengthy debate between Love and Wealth as to which had greater power. This culminated in a combat between six horsemen, ending when Jupiter declared both Love and Wealth to be equally necessary to monarchs.

After that came the grand finale. A curtain slipped to the floor, to reveal a large rock upon which sat eight young girls, Princess Mary in their midst. At each side were four lads carrying torches. As trumpets sounded, Mary and her maidens descended from their rock to salute the King, and then they performed a graceful dance. Laying down their torches, the young men followed them, and soon all were dancing together, the spectators joining in, to celebrate Princess Mary's latest betrothal.

# 2

## THE KING'S TWO WIVES

*A*S HE SAT and watched the dancers that night, resting his injured foot in its black velvet slipper, Henry was probably far more preoccupied with his own matrimonial problems than with the prospect of Mary's distant marriage. His quarrel with Catherine of Aragon over his illegitimate son had been symptomatic of the deepening differences between them, and Henry was obsessed with the thought that he must have a male heir. Moreover, he believed that he now knew why the Queen had been unable to give him the son he so desperately desired. During his studies of the Bible, he had come upon an alarming text. 'If a man should take his brother's wife,' says the Book of Leviticus, 'it is an impurity; he hath uncovered his brother's nakedness; they shall be childless.'

He had married his brother's wife. Catherine had been Prince Arthur's widow. That must be why all his legitimate sons had been born dead or had died in infancy. It was God's punishment. If he was ever to have his Prince of Wales, he would have to put the Queen away and marry someone else. Moreover, he knew exactly who his second wife would be: Anne Boleyn, clever, ambitious, witty Anne, daughter of his old friend, Sir Thomas Boleyn, sister of his former mistress, Mary Boleyn.

Anne was no beauty. Her eyes were too dark, her complexion was too swarthy and her neck too long, but her early years in France had given her sophistication and self-assurance, and she seemed to hold an uncanny fascination for the King. No one else liked her, with her sharp tongue and her malicious, disconcerting sense of humour, and she certainly did not behave as Henry's other lady friends had done. She did not blush and succumb gratefully to his blandishments. Instead, she looked him in the eye and told him in no uncertain terms that she would never consent to be his mistress. If he wanted her in his bed, he would have to marry her and make her Queen of England.

Tester of an early sixteenth-century bedstead with Catherine of Aragon's crowned pomegranate and Henry VIII's Tudor rose. (By courtesy of the Board of Trustees of the Victoria & Albert Museum)

15

*Anne Boleyn*, Mary's first stepmother, by an unknown artist.
(National Portrait Gallery, London)

To Catherine of Aragon, her husband seemed as one bewitched. He told her that he no longer wanted to sleep with her, making the excuse that she was his brother's widow. Instead, he danced attendance on Anne Boleyn, writing her love letters, showering her with gifts and behaving as if he were the supplicant, she the gracious monarch. Catherine tried to ignore it, as she had ignored his mistresses in the past. She sailed about the court as usual, smiling, placid, dignified, giving a serene answer to Henry's rudest remarks, behaving as though nothing were amiss, but privately seething with indignation against the evil woman who was trying to lure her husband away.

No one can say how soon Mary knew that something was wrong. She was

*Above*. Book of Hours belonging to Anne
Boleyn, with a message from her to
Henry VIII:
> By daily proof you shall me find
> To be to you both loving and kind.

(By permission of the British Library)

William Tyndale's English translation of the
New Testament, 1534. This copy belonged to
Anne Boleyn.
(By permission of the British Library)

on the periphery of events, living peacefully in her own household under the care of the Countess of Salisbury, protected from the distasteful stories about the King's infatuation for the 'the Concubine', as Catherine's friends called Anne Boleyn. In the overheated atmosphere of the court, however, gossip travelled quickly and Mary must soon enough have begun to hear the stories, and begun to detect her mother's inner agitation. Catherine never criticised the King, to Mary or to anyone else. As far as she was concerned, he was a good man who had been led astray, and she reserved her hatred for Anne and her associates. Mary, young and impressionable, adopted her mother's attitude as her own. She adored her handsome, indulgent, awe-inspiring father, but she became her mother's ardent partisan and the rift between her parents shattered her former happy confidence. Instead she became nervous, apprehensive and miserable.

Henry's campaign to put away his wife began shortly after the betrothal celebrations at Greenwich. That same spring, Cardinal Wolsey presided over a secret court designed to end the King's marriage without Catherine's knowledge. Pope Clement VII would then be asked to approve the annulment, still without the Queen being told, and so the whole matter would be accomplished without giving her a chance to defend herself. If the royal marriage were null and void, of course, then Mary would be illegitimate.

In the event, this scheme came to nothing. Charles V's army in Italy captured the Pope before the secret court could conclude its deliberations. The Pope would never dare to end the marriage of the Emperor's aunt against her will, and both Henry and Wolsey knew it. The proceedings were abandoned, and the King realised that he would have to find some other way of ridding himself of Catherine.

Urged on by Anne Boleyn, he employed scholars all over Europe to hunt for evidence substantiating his claim that his marriage to his brother's wife was null and void – even though he had obtained a dispensation from the Pope allowing him to marry her in the first place. To his fury, far more people seemed ready to condemn him than to support his cause, and they triumphantly produced a text from the Book of Deuteronomy: 'When brethren dwell together, and one of them dieth without children, the wife of the deceased shall not marry to another, but his brother shall take her and raise up seed for his brother.' In other words, Henry had not committed a mortal sin by marrying Prince Arthur's widow. On the contrary, he had unwittingly obeyed the scriptural instruction.

Finding himself in an impossible position, bullied by Henry and in terror of offending the Emperor, Pope Clement VII used every delaying tactic at his disposal, sending Cardinal Campeggio to hear the case in England with Cardinal Wolsey, but instructing him to procrastinate for as long as he possibly could. As diplomats wrangled, as Catherine refused point-blank to agree that her marriage was null, as scholars pored for hours over theological texts, wrote tracts, made speeches and published whole books about dispensations, degrees of affinity and illegal marriages, Anne Boleyn slowly but surely insinuated herself further into the inner royal circle. By 1529 Henry, Catherine and Anne were existing in a curious ménage à trois at Greenwich, each in separate apartments, Catherine attending audiences and ceremonies with unshakeable dignity, Anne becoming more arrogant by the minute and Henry, caught between two determined women, trying desperately to escape from one and please the other.

This was far more than a domestic quarrel, of course, and the repercussions were as dramatic as they were wide-ranging. In 1530 Cardinal Wolsey fell from power, the victim of Anne's rage because he had delayed too long in procuring the King his divorce, and the entire relationship between the Pope and the English was in jeopardy. Anne was triumphant, more confident than ever now that her enemy had disappeared, 'fiercer than a lioness', said the Emperor's ambassador. As for Catherine, she held on determinedly. 'I have truth and right on my side,' she told Charles V, and although Henry wished 'to live with the woman he has under his roof, without the least particle of shame', she was convinced that if only the Pope would give sentence against him, her husband would come to his senses and everything could be as it was before, as it ought to be.

By this time Mary was a vulnerable adolescent of fifteen, and the emotional tension between her father and her mother was taking its toll. After spending five or six days with the Queen in March 1531, she suffered from such acute indigestion that she could keep down almost nothing that she ate. The situation was intolerable for all of them, and that summer Henry was finally browbeaten by Anne into ending their peculiar way of life. Announcing that they were going hunting, the King and Anne rode away from Windsor, leaving Catherine behind. They did not go back, and Henry never saw his wife again.

He did, however, see Mary. Anne Boleyn was violently jealous of the girl, for she realised the strength of affection between father and daughter. She would dearly have liked to separate them forever but, for all that Henry was anxious to please her, he could not bring himself to sever entirely his connection with his only daughter. That September, in what must have been a prearranged meeting, Mary went out riding and came upon the King and his retinue 'in the fields'. She was perturbed to see that two of Anne's attendants were with him, keeping close to his side, listening avidly to everything that was said.

Henry greeted her stiffly, and after a moment enquired about her health, for he had heard that she had been ill again. She made some suitable reply. At that, he looked upon her more kindly and promised that he would see her more often than he had been doing. He did not invite her to go and stay with him, as had been his habit, but she was not surprised. She knew how Anne Boleyn felt about her and, in any event, she herself had no desire to set foot in the same house as 'the Concubine'.

Despite Henry's apparent softening towards Mary, his campaign of threats and bullying behaviour against Catherine continued unabated. Mother and daughter were not permitted to live together. When Henry had gone off from Windsor, Mary had hurried there to comfort the Queen, but almost at once orders had come telling Catherine that she was to go and live at the More, one of Wolsey's former houses. Mary was sent to Richmond. Soon, Catherine was told to hand over all her jewels, and of course Anne Boleyn was immediately seen wearing them. Even then, the Queen made excuses for her husband. He was like a bull being goaded with lances in the arena, she told the Emperor. 'It is a great pity,' she went on, 'that a person so good and virtuous should be thus deceived and misled every day', and she signed her letter, 'From More, separated from my husband without having ever offended him.'

Realising that he never would extract an annulment from the Pope, Henry decided to break with Rome altogether. Lutheran Anne had been plying him with the writings of the Reformers, and he believed that he had found a new way out of his dilemma. He would set himself up as Supreme Head of the Church of England, and then he could do as he liked.

Sir Thomas More, Wolsey's successor as Lord Chancellor and one of the most admired scholars in Europe, resigned, but even that did not give Henry pause. He seemed to be so set on marrying Anne that he could think of almost nothing else. She had moved into Catherine's apartments now, and as well as giving her the Queen's jewels, he was plying her with other gifts – magnificent hangings and a sumptuous crimson satin bed draped with cloth of gold and silver. In September 1532, on the eve of taking Anne with him on a state visit to France, he created her Marchioness of Pembroke.

Was this her reward for finally agreeing to sleep with him? Historians argue still about the exact time that they began to cohabit, but by the beginning of 1533 she was pregnant. As soon as he knew, Henry married her, in a ceremony so secret that no one is sure precisely where it took place.

On 13 April Anne's marriage to King Henry VIII was publicly announced, and the new Archbishop of Canterbury, Thomas Cranmer, a Boleyn protégé, declared that Henry's first marriage had been invalid from the very start. Messengers rode to tell Catherine of Aragon that she was no longer Queen. In future, she must style herself 'Dowager Princess of Wales'. Anne Boleyn's chamberlain seized Catherine's royal barge and cut her coat of arms from it. Even more hurtfully, Henry demanded that Catherine should hand over the beautiful christening robe she had brought from Spain for her own children. Anne wanted it for her coming infant's baptism. For once, Catherine refused to obey.

At the same time, Mary was told that she must no longer call herself 'Princess'. She was the Lady Mary, the King's bastard daughter and Anne threatened to humble her by making her come to court to be one of her own maids of honour. It was not surprising that Mary fell ill again that summer, so ill that the King allowed her mother's Spanish doctor and apothecary to attend her. Desperate to protect her, Catherine apparently spoke of marrying Mary to the Countess of Salisbury's son, Reginald Pole. A devout, intellectual young man, he was sixteen years older than Mary, but they knew and liked each

*Sir Thomas More, Lord Chancellor of England,* by Holbein.
(The Royal Collection © 1993 Her Majesty The Queen)

Design by Holbein for an archway erected for Anne Boleyn's coronation entry into London, 1533. (Kupferstichkabinett, Staatliche Museen zu Berlin, Preussischer Kulturbesitz: photograph, Jorg P Anders)

other, sharing a similarity of disposition which he was to remark upon, long years later. Mary would 'gladly' have become his wife, it was said, but her father would never have agreed to the match, and nothing came of it.

Instead, Mary went on living in the country, in a state of nervous apprehension. Anne Boleyn's child was born on 7 September 1533; not the son the King so desperately desired, but a daughter, whom he named Elizabeth, after his own mother. As soon as she heard, Mary wrote a consoling letter to Catherine, and their friends rejoiced privately at Henry's supposed discomfiture. However, they dared not show their true feelings and one of the few to risk the King's wrath was the Marchioness of Exeter, who sent both mother and daughter all the latest court news by way of Eustace Chapuys.

Chapuys was the Emperor's ambassador, and it was his duty to report to Brussels everything that happened at the English court. He was deeply sympathetic to the Queen and the Princess, and full of indignation at the way they were being treated. He did everything he could to protect their interests, but there was little he could do to prevent their daily humiliation.

In October, a deputation of Privy Councillors arrived at Beaulieu in Essex, Mary's favourite residence. Chapuys later gave Charles V the details. Henry, the councillors said, had heard that his daughter was still calling herself 'Princess', and that must stop at once. The title belonged not to her, but to his daughter, Elizabeth. Mary remained adamant. She would obey her father until the end of her days, but she really could not renounce the titles, rights and privileges which God, Nature and her own parents had given her. Being the daughter of a King and Queen, putting aside other circumstances, she was rightly called Princess. Nothing would make her either say that she was illegitimate or compromise the position of her mother, whose example she had been determined to follow by placing herself entirely in the hands of God, and bearing with patience her misfortunes.

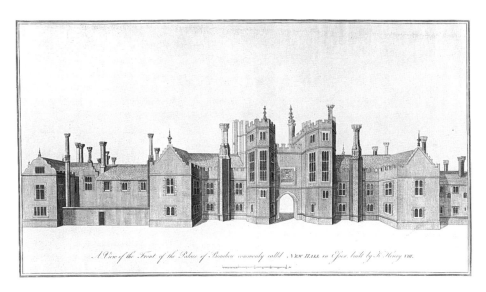

Beaulieu, sometimes called New Hall, Mary's favourite Essex residence, seen in an eighteenth-century engraving by George Vertue.
(Reproduced by courtesy of Essex Record Office)

*Thomas, 3rd Duke of Norfolk*, by Holbein.
(The Royal Collection © 1993 Her Majesty The Queen)

Ignoring this retort, her visitors went on to tell her that they had orders to dismiss most of her household of over one hundred and sixty or so attendants, and that her allowance was to be drastically cut. When she sent messengers to her friend, Chapuys, describing what had happened, he was filled with foreboding. While applauding her courage, he very much feared that if she tried her father's patience too far, Henry would either shut her up in a nunnery or marry her off against her will to a man of low birth. He urged caution, advising her to obey her father's orders. She could, after all, protect her position by signing a protest saying that she was acting under duress.

His advice was timely. In mid-December, Anne Boleyn's uncle, the Duke of Norfolk, rode up to Beaulieu, with a curt and unwelcome message. The infant Princess of Wales, he began, was being taken to Hatfield. Before he could say another word, Mary interrupted. 'That is a title which belongs to me by right and to no one else,' she exclaimed, and when Norfolk went on to tell her that she was to join Elizabeth and live with her as one of her maids of honour, she burst out angrily that this was a strange and unfitting proposal. She said much more, to the same purpose and, when she paused for breath, the Duke snarled that he had not come to dispute, but to see the King's wishes accomplished. Realising that her arguments were having no effect, Mary hurried into her private chamber to copy out the draft protest Chapuys had sent her for just such an occasion as this.

When she emerged half an hour later, she looked round at her distraught servants and said to the Duke, 'Since such is my father's wish, it is not for me to disobey his injunctions, but I beg you to intercede with him that the services of many well-deserving and trusty officers of my household may be rewarded and one year's wages at least given to them.' She also asked how many attendants she might take with her. The Duke retorted that she would find plenty of servants where she was going.

At this rude response, Lady Salisbury stepped forward indignantly and said that she would serve Princess Mary with a large retinue, at her own expense. The Duke brushed the offer angrily aside. Mary might take with her two maids, her tutor, and a little group of gentlemen, but that was all. She was ushered into a plain, leather-covered litter and they set off for Hatfield without more delay.

Arriving at the mansion which was to be Elizabeth's principal residence, the Duke sarcastically asked Mary if she was not pleased to pay court to the Princess. She replied brusquely that she knew of no princess in England other than herself. If the King acknowledged Madame de Pembroke's daughter as his child, she said, just as he acknowledged the Duke of Richmond as his son, then she would treat Elizabeth as a sister, but the girl was certainly not Princess of Wales. Ignoring her remarks, Norfolk led her up to a room near the top of the house and, turning to go, asked if she had any message for the King. 'None,' she replied proudly, 'except that the Princess of Wales, his daughter, asked for his blessing!' Staring at her, the Duke said that he did not dare take such a message. 'Then go away and leave me alone,' Mary exclaimed, and fled to her chamber, where she burst into tears.

Her life had changed completely. From being the loved and petted Princess of Wales, at the centre of her own large household, she was consigned to the attics like a servant, and allowed only one maid to see to her needs. Anne Boleyn's aunt, Lady Shelton, replaced the Countess of Salisbury as her Lady Governess, and several of her former attendants, including her favourite

The Old Palace at Hatfield.
(Photograph, A F Kersting)

cousin, Lady Margaret Douglas, were assigned to Elizabeth instead.

Every day was filled with petty humiliations, and as if that were not trouble enough, she was consumed with anxiety about her mother. She had heard that the Duke of Suffolk had tried to move Catherine to the remote house of Somersham, on the edge of the Fens. Shutting herself in her room, Catherine had refused to go. 'If you wish to take me, you must break down the door,' she had shouted defiantly to the disconcerted Duke. He had retreated, but no doubt he would be back. In the meantime, she managed to send Mary regular messages of advice. Whatever happened, the Princess must never give up her title, never throw doubts on the legality of her mother's marriage and never abandon the Roman Catholic religion.

Furious at the defiance of his wife and daughter, Henry VIII decided to visit Hatfield himself early in 1534. Ostensibly he was going to see the infant Elizabeth, but he also intended to force Mary into submission. When she heard that he was coming, she was filled with excitement. Surely she would be able to speak to him, tell him of her ill-treatment in this house, and make him realise that his so-called wife was persecuting her without his knowledge. Far from receiving her sympathetically, however, Henry gave orders that she was not to come near him. Perhaps he feared that the sight of her might weaken his resolve. Probably Anne, consumed with jealousy, had made him promise not to see his elder daughter.

At any rate, he sent his secretary, Thomas Cromwell, with the Lord Treasurer and the captain of his bodyguard to remonstrate with Mary. As soon as they entered her chamber, she told them scornfully that they were wasting

The Great Hall at Hampton Court, completed in Anne Boleyn's time.
(Photograph, A F Kersting)

Anne Boleyn's Gateway at Hampton Court.
(Photograph, A F Kersting)

*Charles Brandon, 1st Duke of Suffolk*,
Mary's uncle by marriage, by an
unknown artist.
(National Portrait Gallery, London)

their time. She could not, however, resist begging them to let her see her father. They refused. Not to be defeated, she went up to the roof of the palace, and waited. Henry eventually emerged and, glancing up, saw her kneeling there, her hands clasped in supplication. Almost against his will, he nodded and touched his hat, whereupon the courtiers with him bowed reverently to her.

When Henry arrived back at court, he told the French ambassador sternly that he would neither see nor speak to Mary on account of her stubborn and obstinate disobedience to his commands which, he said, she had 'inherited with her Spanish blood'. The ambassador murmured politely that she had been very well brought up, whereupon Henry's eyes filled with easy tears and he could not help praising her accomplishments. Anne Boleyn soon stiffened his resolve, however. Instructions were given that Mary was no longer to be allowed to have breakfast in her own room. She must eat in the hall like everyone else, and for good measure Anne sent word to her aunt that if Mary persisted in calling herself 'Princess', Lady Shelton was 'to slap her face as the cursed bastard that she was'.

Early in March, Anne went to Hatfield herself and, so Chapuys heard, invited Mary to meet her and honour her 'as the Queen, which she was'. Were she to do so, the King would treat Mary as well and perhaps even better than he had ever done. Mary's reply, that she knew not of 'any other Queen in England than Madame her mother,' but that she would be grateful if the King's mistress interceded on her behalf, was hardly conciliatory. Anne rode back to London in a fury, telling her friends she would 'put down that proud Spanish blood' and do her worst. A few days later, the Duke of Norfolk seized Mary's jewels and all her best clothes.

It was not surprising that she was feeling furious and upset by the time the household left Hatfield a few days later. It was a complicated operation. Horses were brought from the stables, servants hurried about with bundles of clothing and household equipment, and the various ladies and gentlemen courtiers took their places in the cavalcade, each in careful order of precedence. Lady Shelton installed herself in a magnificent, horse-drawn litter at the head of the procession, with Princess Elizabeth on her lap. At last, everyone was ready to go; everyone, that is, except Mary. Her much plainer litter waited in second place, and that, of course, was the trouble. She was determined not to yield precedence to her father's bastard daughter.

Finally, Lady Shelton beckoned to a group of gentlemen and gave them angry instructions. They disappeared back into the palace. An ominous silence followed, to be broken by the sound of muffled screams. The men emerged again, dragging with them a small, struggling figure. Lady Mary's fair face was flushed, her eyes were red with weeping and she still gasped out her defiance, but they ignored her protests. Pulling her over to her litter, they flung her inside, and within seconds the procession was moving off, on its way to the next residence on the royal circuit.

Mary's defiance was not merely the outcome of her own turbulent emotions, of course. As Chapuys observed, 'the Queen her mother and some of her friends have for some time been thinking that it was better for the Princess to act thus and show her teeth to the King'. He himself was of a different opinion, for he feared that she would further damage her own position and that Henry would lose his temper, 'playing her some bad trick in order to please his mistress Anne, who never ceases day and night plotting against her'.

Mary paid little heed to the ambassador's advice, for it seemed to her that upholding her own and her mother's position was more important than any personal danger. Catherine still clung to the belief that once the Pope publicly condemned Henry, the King would come to his senses, and that spring the long-awaited news came. On 24 March 1534, the Pope finally declared that Henry VIII's marriage to Catherine of Aragon was valid and always had been. Mary was overjoyed when Chapuys sent a messenger to tell her. She could not have been more delighted had he sent her a million pounds, she declared – but it was too late, Henry was not going to turn back now, and by the middle of May even Catherine was forced to accept that the papal sentence would not restore Henry to her.

For the past two years, in fact, Parliament had been enacting legislation securing the King's position as Supreme Head of the Church in England, and severing all ties with Rome. Revenues no longer went to the Holy See, there were to be no more appeals from church courts to Rome and Henry had been given the power to reform all the religious houses in England. Moreover, an Act of Succession stated that Henry's marriage to Catherine was null and void, and that his children by Anne Boleyn would succeed him on the throne. Every subject in the land was to take an oath promising to observe the act, and anyone daring to criticise the King or his marriage to Anne would be charged with high treason.

Six weeks after the papal sentence, the King sent a deputation to Catherine, demanding that she take the oath. She refused, of course, and she was at once removed to Kimbolton Castle, near Peterborough. Rejecting her new title of 'Princess Dowager', she shut herself in the apartments assigned to her with a few of her faithful Spanish servants and refused to see anyone else. She was ready for martyrdom, she said, adding that her greatest fear was not for herself; it was for her daughter.

Mary's enemies lost no time in telling her about the new Act of Succession and they repeated current rumours that Henry was threatening to execute his elder daughter. Each day she waited apprehensively for another royal deputation to arrive, but nothing happened. Alternating between terror and defiance, she was writing to Chapuys as many as three times a day, begging for his advice. He urged her, as he always had done, not to irritate her father further, although he acknowledged that she should not appear too submissive, lest the King think she was losing courage and bully her even more.

She continued her campaign of refusing to yield precedence to her half-sister, counting it a triumph on one occasion when she was able to set off first in her litter and so arrive at Greenwich in time to seize the seat of honour in the royal barge before Elizabeth appeared. Inevitably, she experienced a nervous reaction to all the excitement, and that autumn she was seriously ill again. She was also suffering from her 'usual trouble', which seems to have been pre-menstrual tension and dysmenorrhoea. Doctors prescribed riding and other vigorous exercise in such cases, and when that did not provoke menstruation, they bled the patient. It was not surprising that she was thin and very pale. Dr Butts, sent by Henry VIII to examine her, enraged the King by telling him that her trouble was 'partly the result of the worry and extreme annoyance to which she had been subjected'. 'Is it not a great misfortune,' Henry whined, 'that my daughter should be so obstinate, and persevere in a line of conduct that prevents my treating her as I should wish and as she deserves?'

*William Butts*, one of the royal doctors who attended Mary, by Holbein.
(National Portrait Gallery, London)

*John Fisher, Bishop of Rochester*, Catherine of Aragon's staunch defender, by Holbein, 1535.
(The Royal Collection © 1993 Her Majesty The Queen)

*Catherine of Aragon*, about 1525, a miniature attributed to Horenbout.
(National Portrait Gallery, London)

He refused all pleas that Mary should be allowed to go and live with her mother, who promised to save any expense by nursing her, sharing her bed and sitting up with her when necessary. Catherine, said the King, was 'a proud and intractable woman', and, were she to take it into her head to favour her daughter, she might well take the field, raise assemblies of men, and carry on war against him 'as openly and fiercely as Queen Isabella her mother did in Spain'.

Mary did recover again, but the following spring she seemed to be in greater danger than ever. Three Carthusians and two other clerics were executed at Tyburn in May 1535 for refusing to take the oath, three more Carthusians died on 19 June and, a few days after that, one of Catherine's most energetic defenders, John Fisher, Bishop of Rochester, was executed. Sir Thomas More followed him to the scaffold. It seemed certain that Catherine and her daughter would be next to die. Mary made desperate plans to escape to the Continent, but the Emperor pointed out that she would never be allowed to get away. She and her mother should take the oath rather than risk their lives, he said.

Catherine would never have done so, whatever the danger. She continued to speak calmly of martyrdom, but at the beginning of December she fell seriously ill with vomiting and violent pains in the stomach. Her physician, Miguel de La Sa, her apothecary, Juan de Soto, and his assistant, Philip Grenacre, did what they could for her, and as Christmas approached, she seemed better. She had a serious relapse on 26 December, however, and Eustace Chapuys decided that he must see her, whatever the consequences for himself might be.

He arrived at Kimbolton to find Catherine so weak that she could not even sit up in bed. She had not slept for six nights, she told him, but she was overjoyed to see him and he tried to comfort her by telling her that the King had been very sorry to hear of her illness – a kind invention of his own devising. He spent four days with her and then, since she seemed better, he rode reluctantly back to London, leaving one of his attendants with her.

That evening, she seemed to be recovering. She even teased Chapuys' servant, who was well-known for his humorous disposition, and on Twelfth Night she was able to comb and tie back her hair without help, but the following day she suffered another relapse and she realised that she was dying. After hearing Mass, she dictated her will to Dr de La Sa, making provision for her servants, arranging for a pilgrimage and for Masses in her memory, and bequeathing to her daughter, Mary, her furs, and 'the collar of gold which I brought out of Spain'.

Summoning her remaining strength, she signed the will and then she told de La Sa to write down her last letter to Henry VIII, 'My most dear lord, king and husband'. Urging him to safeguard his soul, she told him, 'For my part, I pardon you everything, and I wish to devoutly pray God that He will pardon you also. For the rest, I commend unto you our daughter Mary, beseeching you to be a good father unto her, as I have heretofore desired. I entreat you also, on behalf of my maids, to give them marriage portions, which is not much, they being but three. For all my other servants I solicit the wages due them, and a year more, lest they be unprovided. Lastly, I make this vow, that mine eyes desire you above all things.' At ten in the morning she received extreme unction from her chaplain, Jorge de Athequa, Bishop of Llandaff, responding to the questions of the ritual in a clear and audible voice. She died at two o'clock that afternoon.

# 3

## AN OBEDIENT DAUGHTER

'*THANK GOD!*' exclaimed Henry VIII when he heard the news, 'We are now free from any fear of war!' He had always dreaded the thought that the Emperor might invade England on Catherine of Aragon's behalf, but now that danger had been removed. Next morning he appeared clad in bright yellow, from head to toe, as a visible sign of his rejoicing. Anne Boleyn was more ambivalent in her response. She had longed for the time when she would be the unchallenged Queen of England but, now that it had come, she could not stop thinking that she, too, might one day die a lonely and discarded death.

She had seen the way Henry looked at pale, meek Jane Seymour, and she knew what that look meant. At one time, a word from Anne would have brought him running back to her, wringing his hands, begging her forgiveness and pleading for a kind word, but his former ardour was quenched, replaced by cold disdain. Worse still, he was telling people that Anne had lured him into marriage by witchcraft. Did he mean to put her away, as he had put away Catherine? Assailed by terrible doubts, she reassured herself with one thought. She was pregnant. If she could give the King his longed-for son, then she was safe.

Mary did not learn that her mother was dead until four days later, when Lady Shelton came and told her the news, brusquely, without preamble. When she had recovered a little from the shock, she pleaded for a visit from her mother's physician and apothecary. Reluctantly, Henry agreed to her request and Dr de La Sa and Juan de Soto spent two days with her, giving her a full account of her mother's last hours. They probably brought with them the precious memento which Catherine had bequeathed to her daughter. This was a plain gold necklace, apparently of relatively low value since it was not set with jewels, but which was said to contain a piece of the True Cross. That, combined with the fact that it had been her mother's, made the necklace doubly important to Mary. She was greatly distressed when Thomas Cromwell, hearing of its existence, demanded that she send it to him. However, Cromwell lost interest when he discovered that the necklace was of little intrinsic value and he returned it to her.

Mary did not attend her mother's funeral, nor would she allow Eustace Chapuys to participate. Instead of holding a ceremony appropriate to a Queen of England, Henry VIII had given orders that his first wife was to be buried with the rank of Dowager Princess of Wales. To attend the service would have been to give tacit recognition to this reduction in her mother's status, said Mary, and she was determined not to condone the insult.

Catherine was buried in Peterborough Cathedral on 29 January 1536, some distance from the high altar, and that same day Anne Boleyn suffered a miscarriage. According to her women, her baby would indeed have been a boy, and Henry VIII was beside himself with rage. Marching into Anne's bedchamber, he glared down at her and snarled, 'I see that God will not give me male children. When you are up I will speak to you', then he turned on his heel and strode out. Anne quickly regained her strength and she got up, and joked and laughed and ordered her servants about more imperiously than ever; but she was afraid.

Was that why she suddenly sent a strangely conciliatory message to Mary? If the girl submitted and took the oath, Anne said, she would at once become her warmest friend, a second mother to her. Moreover, if Mary wished to come to court, she would be excused from acting as a train-bearer to the Queen. She could walk by her side, like an equal. Mary refused the offer scornfully. She looked elsewhere for friendship and support. With her mother gone, she was

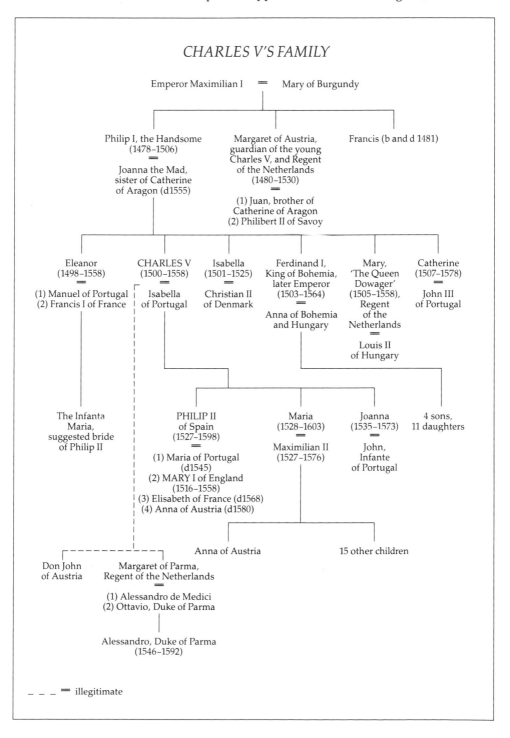

## CHARLES V'S FAMILY

Emperor Maximilian I = Mary of Burgundy

Philip I, the Handsome (1478–1506) = Joanna the Mad, sister of Catherine of Aragon (d1555)

Margaret of Austria, guardian of the young Charles V, and Regent of the Netherlands (1480–1530) = (1) Juan, brother of Catherine of Aragon (2) Philibert II of Savoy

Francis (b and d 1481)

Eleanor (1498–1558) = (1) Manuel of Portugal (2) Francis I of France

CHARLES V (1500–1558) = Isabella of Portugal

Isabella (1501–1525) = Christian II of Denmark

Ferdinand I, King of Bohemia, later Emperor (1503–1564) = Anna of Bohemia and Hungary

Mary, 'The Queen Dowager' (1505–1558), Regent of the Netherlands = Louis II of Hungary

Catherine (1507–1578) = John III of Portugal

The Infanta Maria, suggested bride of Philip II

PHILIP II of Spain (1527–1598) = (1) Maria of Portugal (d1545) (2) MARY I of England (1516–1558) (3) Elisabeth of France (d1568) (4) Anna of Austria (d1580)

Maria (1528–1603) = Maximilian II (1527–1576)

Joanna (1535–1573) = John, Infante of Portugal

4 sons, 11 daughters

Anna of Austria

15 other children

Don John of Austria

Margaret of Parma, Regent of the Netherlands = (1) Alessandro de Medici (2) Ottavio, Duke of Parma

Alessandro, Duke of Parma (1546–1592)

_ _ _ = illegitimate

31

*Jane Seymour*, Mary's second stepmother, by Holbein.
(Kunsthistorisches Museum, Vienna)

Catherine of Aragon's grave in Peterborough Cathedral. Her tomb was destroyed in 1643 by Cromwell's men. (By kind permission of the Dean and Chapter, Peterborough Cathedral: photograph, © Pitkin Pictorials Ltd)

*Charles V as Master of the World*, a copy by Peter Paul Rubens of a lost painting of about 1529 by Parmigianino. (Residenzgalerie, Salzburg)

relying more than ever on the Emperor for protection, confident that in him she had a formidable friend.

Charles V, she knew, was no longer the gangling, unimpressive youth of her childhood recollection. He had broadened out, concealed his unfortunate Habsburg chin with a neatly-trimmed beard and become a man of truly imperial dignity and presence. A shrewd judge of character and an experienced observer of the ways of the world, he was astute in his dealings with monarchs and ambassadors, statesmen and courtiers. He genuinely wanted to bring peace to his vast domains and in pursuit of this aim he deployed his female relatives throughout Europe. His wife, the Empress Isabella, ruled Spain for him, and his capable, energetic sister Mary, the Dowager Queen of Hungary, was governing the Low Countries on his behalf. They were not mere pawns in the diplomatic game, to be used without consideration for their own feelings. They were effective, capable women, whom he treated with respect. He would never have behaved towards them as Henry behaved towards Catherine and Mary.

Charles and his family were concerned about the situation in England, not least because, if Henry VIII broke with them entirely, he and the French might get together and cut the communications between Spain and the Netherlands. They had also felt a personal sympathy for Catherine of Aragon's plight, and Charles and the Queen Dowager had both written to her during her last illness. Their letters had arrived too late to be given to Catherine, so Chapuys had passed them on to Mary instead and she treasured them, finding in these messages a real source of solace.

Design by Holbein for a chimneypiece, probably for Henry VIII's palace of Bridewell. (Reproduced by courtesy of the Trustees of the British Museum)

She felt, indeed, that these kind friends would do everything they could to protect her interests, and her dearest wish was that the Emperor should invade England, drive out Anne Boleyn and put everything to rights again. Unfortunately for Mary, Charles V had his own priorities and they were not hers. Seated in his palace in Brussels, surrounded by reports from his ambassadors, letters from his wife, memoranda from the Queen Dowager, petitions, draft treaties, accounts and commissions, he had more to think about than the difficulties of his English cousin.

He pitied her, of course, and he deplored the way she was being treated, but there was little he could do. He had far too many problems of his own to occupy his mind: the spread of Protestantism in the Empire; the nefarious dealings of his old enemy, Francis I of France; the war in Italy, and his own financial exhaustion. All else apart, he really could not interfere between Henry VIII and Mary. A father had absolute authority over a daughter and even an Emperor had no right to meddle. As long as Henry was alive, Charles was far more likely to offer Mary good advice than to intervene directly.

Bombarded with her desperate letters, Eustace Chapuys felt that he must act swiftly to save her, and he pleaded with the Emperor to let him spirit Mary over to Brussels. Charles was discouraging. Ever the realist, he pointed out that she would never be able to slip out of the country undetected, and in any event her presence at his own court would be a dreadful diplomatic embarrassment. It would be far better if she could find some right-thinking, Roman Catholic husband. His own brother-in-law, Dom Luis of Portugal, would be an excellent choice. She could then leave England with her father's blessing, and her future would be secure.

Mary herself seemed strangely ambivalent about Chapuys' suggestions. She was constantly assuring him of her ardent desire to escape and yet, when he tried to make practical plans, she was evasive, raising all manner of practical difficulties. He began to wonder if she was really serious. It was almost as if she wanted to stay in England after all, he thought, and he was probably right. Apart from her reluctance to leave her friends, she had had word of exciting developments at court.

For several weeks past, Anne Boleyn's enemies had been plotting the Queen's downfall, and Mary was receiving secret messages from Sir Nicholas Carew and the other conspirators, giving assurances and holding out hopes. There was talk of persuading the King to divorce 'the Concubine' so that he could marry Jane Seymour instead, then suddenly, before anyone expected it, Anne was arrested. The King had made a dreadful discovery, it seemed. His wife had taken lovers, including even her own brother, Viscount Rochford, and together they had conspired to murder Henry. They were tried for treason, and condemned to death. On 17 May, Anne's marriage was pronounced null and void, and two days later she was executed on Tower Green. Henry VIII immediately announced his betrothal to Jane Seymour.

Suddenly, Mary's prospects were enormously improved. She found herself the centre of attention, receiving congratulations and messages of goodwill from all those who, for months, had been too frightened to have any dealings with her. Surely her father would invite her back to court and restore her to her proper place? She waited eagerly, but no invitation came, no kindly message, nothing. Gradually her happy confidence faded and she realised with a sinking sense of disbelief that her father must still be angry with her. What was she to do? For once, the Emperor could not help, and so she turned to

*Thomas Cromwell, 1st Earl of Essex*, after Holbein.
(National Portrait Gallery, London)

Thomas Cromwell. She had never trusted him before, this devious ally of 'the Concubine', but since Anne's downfall she had begun to see him in a different light. He was Henry's principal adviser. He would know what the King wanted.

His reply was brisk and unequivocal. Of course the King was still angry with her, and would remain so until she submitted to him, recognised that her mother's marriage had been invalid and that he was Head of the Church of England. Cromwell helpfully drafted a letter for her to send to her father, but by the time she had altered the wording to quieten her conscience, it was not what was required at all. Henry had no desire to read that she would obey him 'next to God'. He expected an unconditional submission. He did not even acknowledge her letter.

After a week, Mary wrote again, begging for an answer, and she sent another letter two days after that. 'I assure you, by the faith I owe to God, I have done the uttermost that my conscience will suffer me', she protested to Cromwell. He was unsympathetic. He had told her what she must do. Sooner or later she was going to have to submit. Even the King's new wife, Jane, had failed to make Henry soften his attitude. When she had begged him to restore

Mary without further delay, he had told her rudely that she must be out of her senses to think of such a thing, and that she ought to study the welfare and exaltation of her own children, if she had any.

A few days after that conversation, the Duke of Norfolk, the Earl of Sussex and the Bishop of Chichester rode down to the house of Hunsdon, where Mary was staying. The King required her to answer two questions, she was told. Would she recognise him as Supreme Head of the Church, and would she agree that her parents' marriage had been invalid? She would not.

Cromwell was exasperated. 'I think you are the most obstinate woman that ever was,' he wrote. Two of her friends, Sir Anthony Browne and Sir Francis Bryan, were arrested and Lady Hussey, wife of her former chamberlain, was sent to the Tower for trying to speak in her favour. Eustace Chapuys, convinced that she would follow if she continued to resist, sent her a stream of messages telling her that the Emperor wanted her to obey her father, to save her life. If she would not do it for her own sake, then she must do it for England. Were she to be executed for treason, the nation would be torn apart by civil war.

Unable to sleep, tormented by toothache and neuralgia, Mary scarcely knew what to do. She tried to remember how her own mother had met the threat of death with serenity, saying that she welcomed martyrdom, but Catherine was gone now and she herself was only twenty, alone and afraid. She could never betray her mother, and yet her present life was intolerable. Not only did she dread the thought of what might happen to her, the prospect of a return to her former comfortable position as the King's favoured daughter was too seductive to be ignored. On 22 June she signed her father's articles without reading them, and she wrote him a covering letter saying that she submitted to him without reservation.

Almost at once she was tortured by guilt at having betrayed her mother and her Church, but at least her letter did have the desired effect. This time, her father replied. He sent her a gracious message, with his paternal blessing, and on 6 July he and Queen Jane visited her. They spent the entire day together,

*Henry Fitzroy, Duke of Richmond*, Henry VIII's illegitimate son, painted by Horenbout towards the end of the Duke's life.
(The Royal Collection © 1993 Her Majesty The Queen)

and Henry and she had a long, private conversation which she afterwards described to Chapuys.

The King had been very kind, she said. He had spoken to her quite sharply about her past disobedience, it was true, criticising her reliance on the Emperor and questioning her about her dealings with him, but that said, he had pressed a note for about a thousand crowns into her hand, telling her not to worry about money for her private expenses, promising to augment her household and saying that she should come and live at court as soon as Jane had been crowned. The Queen herself was very friendly, speaking to her affectionately and presenting her with a beautiful diamond ring. They took dinner together in Mary's chamber, and then they left, with further promises and expressions of good will.

There had been no mention of restoring her title of Princess, but Mary's renewed importance was undeniable, especially after her half-brother, the Duke of Richmond, died of tuberculosis on 23 July, at the age of eighteen. A week or two later, Henry told Mary that he might make her his heiress, for he was getting old, he said, and he would probably not have any children by Jane. Once he had taken a decision about that, he would speak to her about the

*Henry VIII dining in his Privy Chamber*, by an unknown artist. (Reproduced by courtesy of the Trustees of the British Museum)

possibility of her marrying Dom Luis. Moreover, now that she was in favour again, Francis I was showing an interest. He wanted her as a bride for one of his sons.

Along with this encouragement, however, came a distressing command. She was to write to the Emperor, the Pope and the Queen Dowager, telling them that she now accepted the invalidity of her mother's marriage and her father's position as Supreme Head of the Church. She could hardly bear to do it, yet having come thus far she could not refuse. With anguish and with secret messages to the recipients explaining that she was writing under duress, she penned the required letters and Henry was graciously pleased.

He invited her to court, and by the end of November she was dining with him each day, at his own table. The King was once more her loving father, so it seemed. He was not going to grant her the title of Princess, but she was to live in a style befitting his elder daughter. He allowed her more than forty attendants and permitted her to call in Dr de La Sa and Juan de Soto whenever she was unwell. She had chaplains, grooms, gentlemen and gentlewomen, that customary companion of royal ladies, a female fool, Jane, and an acrobat named Lucrece the Tumbler.

Henry was generous in other ways too, and he saw that she had more than enough money to spend on fine clothes, which she loved. Soon she was ordering new outfits to wear at court: richly coloured and patterned French gowns with tight-fitting bodices, full sleeves and wide skirts over embroidered kirtles. Her hoods were trimmed with gem-set bands and Henry augmented her fine collection of jewellery with frequent gifts. She had gold collars set with rubies and diamonds, intricate brooches, delicate earrings, bracelets, rings and jewelled girdles. Already, in December 1536, Blaise the Embroiderer was decorating the sleeves of one of her gowns and the goldsmith was lengthening jewelled borders which Henry had given her to wear round the necks of her dresses.

On 12 October 1537 Queen Jane gave birth to a son, and Mary was delighted. She felt no qualm, it seems, at the thought that she had been displaced as heir to the throne. She gave forty shillings in alms that day, and ordered a new kirtle of cloth of silver for the christening. She was godmother at the ceremony, which took place in the royal chapel at Hampton Court three days later. Elizabeth was there, too, and when the Prince had been baptised Edward and the service was over, Mary and her small sister left the chapel together, walking hand in hand. Now that Elizabeth was also deemed illegitimate, it was easier for Mary to accept her. The child was scarcely more than a baby still, but she was precocious and amusing, and when they played together Mary could almost forget that the little girl was Anne Boleyn's daughter.

The King had his son and heir at last, but his triumph was short-lived, for Jane died of puerperal fever when Prince Edward was twelve days old. Mary was too ill to attend the preliminary mourning services, and her friend, the Marchioness of Exeter, had to take her place, but she had offerings made at each of the thirteen daily Masses at Hampton Court and Windsor for the Queen's soul, and she was able to act as chief mourner when Jane was buried in the choir of St George's Chapel, Windsor on 12 November.

Her sadness was relieved a little when Lady Seymour sent three of her daughters with their nurses to visit her at Windsor. Mary loved small children, and one of these little girls was her god-daughter. She was, indeed, in great

The Chapel Royal, Hampton Court, where Prince Edward was christened.
(Historic Royal Palaces/HMSO: photograph, Clive Friend)

*Grace Newport*, wife of Sir Henry Parker and friend of Mary, by Holbein.
(The Royal Collection © 1993 Her Majesty The Queen)

*John Godsalve*, one of Mary's East Anglian friends, by Holbein.
(The Royal Collection © 1993 Her Majesty The Queen)

demand as a godmother, for many of her friends were young, married couples of about her own age. During her first winter back at court she had kept John of Antwerp, the goldsmith, busy making brooches and pendants for her new godchildren, the sons and daughters of Lady Carew, Mr Outon, Lady Parker, Lady Seymour, Mr Godsalve and Mr Sherbourne. Not only did she attend the christenings in person, but she made a point of visiting the babies afterwards, making generous gifts of money to their nurses and to the midwives who had brought them into the world.

Many of these children were the sons and daughters of long-standing friends. Lady Seymour, for example, was the wife of Queen Jane's brother Edward, and although many people disliked her for her sharp tongue and her forthright opinions, she and Mary enjoyed each other's company. When they were apart, Lady Seymour could be relied upon to send a stream of homely little gifts of quince pies, or cheeses from her dairy.

Another regular companion was a friend from childhood days, Elizabeth Carew. Elizabeth was the daughter of Mary's original governess, Lady Bryan, and there was a double connection, for her husband, Sir Nicholas Carew, had been one of Anne Boleyn's principal adversaries during the final months of her life. Lady Kingston, wife of the Lieutenant of the Tower of London, and Margaret Bacon, wife of the King's physician, Dr Butts, were favourite ladies-in-waiting, and Jane Guildford and her ambitious husband, Sir John Dudley, were often to be found in Mary's company.

She gossiped with these congenial friends, played cards with Lady Carew, Sir William Kingston and Lady Seymour, and gambled away small sums of money as royal ladies always did. She lost money not only at cards but in wagers, sometimes making minor personal items the stake: frontlets, for instance, the decorative bands worn across the forehead. On one occasion, she had a wager with one of her ladies with a breakfast as the prize. Less excitingly, she and her women companions also did a good deal of embroidery, keeping John Hayes busy drawing designs for them to sew on the coverings of cushions and boxes.

Music was another continuing pleasure. Although more than ten years had

*Margaret Bacon*, lady-in-waiting to Mary and wife of the royal physician, William Butts, by Holbein.
(The Royal Collection © 1993 Her Majesty The Queen)

passed since Mary had first impressed her father with her musical accomplishments, she now employed Mr Paston to teach her to play the virginals and took lute lessons from Philip van Wilder of the King's Privy Chamber. Many of the small payments recorded in her accounts were to Mr Cowts, who regularly came to court to mend her virginals, to the King's musicians and to the minstrels employed in other households.

Sometimes, there were more unusual diversions. Morris dancers might come to perform for her, and John Heywood, one of her father's favourite entertainers, not only played the virginals for her but amused her with diverting stories and organised children into performing little plays for her. He had even written a poem, when she was eighteen, describing how:

> Her colour comes and goes
> With such a goodly grace
> More ruddy than the rose
> Within her lively face.

Mary enjoyed archery, and she still rode frequently for the sake of her health, and hunted. She had a special servant, Christopher, to look after her greyhounds. Travelling took up a good deal of her time, for she was constantly on the move, not only between the principal royal residences such as Richmond, Greenwich and St James's Palace, but to other royal houses outside London: Hunsdon, Ampthill, the More and Woodstock. In August and September she went on her own royal progress, taking along tents to shelter her retinue when the places where she stopped did not have adequate accommodation.

Wherever she went, she was greeted with enthusiasm and, particularly in the summertime, she could expect a delightful miscellany of presents: bucks dispatched by Thomas Cromwell and Sir Nicholas Carew, six herons from Lord Cobham, cakes from the Bishop of Carlisle and a parrot from Lady Derby. Not all the donors were of high rank, of course. Ordinary people were equally attentive, arriving to hand in baskets of fish they had caught, dishes of butter they had made, apples and pears from their orchards, chickens, strawberries

Brooke L.ᵈ Cobham.

*George Brooke, 9th Baron Cobham,* another of Mary's friends, by Holbein.
(The Royal Collection © 1993 Her Majesty The Queen)

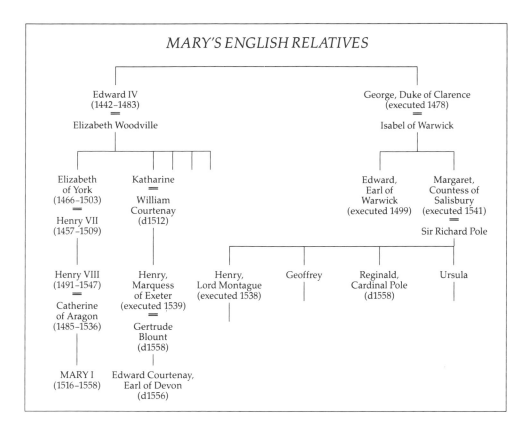

## MARY'S ENGLISH RELATIVES

Edward IV
(1442–1483)
=
Elizabeth Woodville

George, Duke of Clarence
(executed 1478)
=
Isabel of Warwick

Elizabeth
of York
(1466–1503)
=
Henry VII
(1457–1509)

Katharine
=
William
Courtenay
(d1512)

Edward,
Earl of
Warwick
(executed 1499)

Margaret,
Countess of
Salisbury
(executed 1541)
=
Sir Richard Pole

Henry VIII
(1491–1547)
=
Catherine
of Aragon
(1485–1536)

Henry,
Marquess
of Exeter
(executed 1539)
=
Gertrude
Blount
(d1558)

Henry,
Lord Montague
(executed 1538)

Geoffrey

Reginald,
Cardinal Pole
(d1558)

Ursula

MARY I
(1516–1558)

Edward Courtenay,
Earl of Devon
(d1556)

and cream. Thus did they show their sympathy for her and their remembrance of Queen Catherine.

Neither she nor they could forget what had gone before, and even if she had been able to put her mother's troubles out of her mind, there were always present reminders of the consequences of the King's wrath. Her favourite cousin, beautiful, witty Lady Margaret Douglas, was imprisoned in the Tower by the King when she dared to become engaged without his permission. She was moved to more comfortable confinement at Syon House when she fell ill, but she was not released until her fiancé died in the Tower of a fever.

Even more tragic was the treatment accorded to Mary's godmother and governess, the Countess of Salisbury. When the Countess's son, Reginald Pole, was unwise enough to write a long and vehement book condemning the ecclesiastical policies of his former patron, Henry VIII, the King was furious. Reginald was on the Continent, so he was out of reach. The King tried to have him kidnapped and brought back to England, but his efforts failed and the Pope made the situation much worse by tactlessly making Reginald a cardinal. Beside himself with rage, Henry decided to wreak vengeance on the rest of the Pole family.

Pole's two brothers were sent to the Tower, along with the small son of one of them and their friends, the Marquis and Marchioness of Exeter. The Marquis and the elder brother were executed for treason and the little boy was never seen again. The Marchioness and the younger brother were eventually released, but by that time the Countess herself had been charged with treason.

Intensive interrogation failed to make her incriminate herself, and so Thomas Cromwell decided to provide some damning evidence. A white silk

*Anne of Cleves*, Mary's third stepmother, by an unknown artist. (By courtesy of the Board of Trustees of the Victoria & Albert Museum)

*Katherine Parr*, Mary's fifth and final stepmother, painted about 1545 by an unknown artist. (National Portrait Gallery, London)

*Edward VI as a child*, painted by Holbein, about 1538. (Andrew W Mellon Collection © 1993 National Gallery of Art, Washington DC)

44

*A Lady, Princess Mary*, by Holbein.
(The Royal Collection © 1993 Her Majesty The Queen)

coat was produced in court, the kind of garment worn over a suit of armour. It had been found among Lady Salisbury's possessions, so it was said and, although it looked innocent enough, the design embroidered upon it showed its sinister intent. The Pole emblem of the pansy was intertwined with the marigold, Mary's symbol. This clearly showed, the prosecutor said, that the Countess was plotting to marry Mary to her son, overthrow Henry and restore the old religion. Condemned to death, Lady Salisbury was held prisoner in the Tower for a further two miserable years before she was finally executed, at the age of almost seventy. She went to the block calmly in May 1541, protesting her innocence and urging the onlookers to say special prayers for her beloved godchild, the Lady Mary.

By this time, Henry VIII had married again. In January 1540, he had taken a new wife, Anne of Cleves, and in her, Mary found a friend. A year older than herself, the German girl was gauche, ingenuous and eager to please. The fact that she was a Lutheran does not seem to have mattered to Mary. They shared a certain innocence of outlook, as well as an enthusiasm for needlework, and presumably they did not discuss religion.

Unfortunately, the King and Anne were not so compatible. In fact, the first time he saw her, Henry took such a violent dislike to her that he refused to consummate the marriage. Anne did not realise that anything was amiss. After all, she said in bewilderment, they lay in the same bed together and he kissed her goodnight. That summer, ignoring her protests, he had the marriage annulled on the somewhat insubstantial grounds that she had once been tentatively engaged to someone else. Nor did he stop at ridding himself of his wife. He executed Thomas Cromwell, who had arranged the match.

Anne's fate was less dramatic. Henry indicated that she was free to do as she wished. Everyone expected her to retire from England in mortification, but she did not. Instead she stayed, as a respected member of the royal family. Mary and she rode in state processions together and exchanged regular messages and gifts. Not only did they like each other: soon, they were united in their abhorrence of Henry's fifth wife, Catherine Howard. A cousin of Anne Boleyn, Catherine was distinctly reminiscent of her in both appearance and manner. Lively and volatile, she had attracted the King's attention the very first time he met her, and they were secretly married in the same month as the annulment, July 1540.

Mary was appalled, and for once she almost returned to her old, defiant manner. At the beginning of December the new Queen was complaining that her elder stepdaughter did not treat her with sufficient deference. There was a quarrel too, when Catherine apparently removed two of Mary's favourite maids of honour. Amidst growing signs of the King's wrath, Mary hastily sent the Queen such a handsome New Year's gift that both she and the King were mollified, and soon afterwards they paid a visit to the house where Mary and Edward were staying.

When Henry invited Mary to come to court the following spring, Catherine accepted the situation with a reasonably good grace, but the very vivacity which had attracted the King was to be her undoing. In November 1541 Henry discovered that she had not been a virgin when he married her, and the familiar sad sequence of events followed. She was consigned to the Tower and the following February she was beheaded. Henry sank into self-pitying gloom, while Mary fell seriously ill. The details of her sickness are not known, but her life appeared to be in danger and her father anxiously sent his physicians to tend her. Possibly the cause was physical, but the manner of Catherine's death must have brought back all too vividly the last days of Anne Boleyn and the deep emotional upset of that time.

Fortunately both for himself and his children, Henry made a much better choice when he took a sixth wife. Katherine Parr was four years older than Mary. Her mother had been one of Catherine of Aragon's favourite ladies, and she and Mary had known each other in childhood. Since those days, Katherine had been twice married to older men and on both occasions had been left a childless widow.

A calm, gracious lady with a round, pretty face, she seemed the ideal consort for the ageing king. No longer the athletic, magnificent monarch of his youth, Henry was by now seriously overweight, troubled by a painful ulcer in his leg, uncertain of temper and given to terrifying outbursts of rage. According to court gossip, Katherine was deeply in love with Thomas Seymour, one of Queen Jane's brothers, but when the King decided to marry her she had to set aside her own feelings and obey. Mary, Elizabeth and Edward were among the eighteen specially invited guests at Hampton Court when Bishop Stephen Gardiner married the couple on 12 July 1543.

# 4

## KING EDWARD

*A*FTER HER father's wedding, Mary spent a few weeks with her new stepmother. Queen Katherine was an enthusiastic patron of the Reformed Church and its scholars, gathering round her a group of noted classicists and theologians but, as with Anne of Cleves, the religious difference did not cloud Mary's relationship with her. They were, and remained, close friends. Later that summer, Mary went to her mother's former home at the More, moving on to Grafton, Woodstock and eventually spending a little time at Dunstable. In September, one of the Lord Admiral's gentlemen brought her 'ten pairs of Spanish gloves from a Duchess in Spain', a fleeting indication of the continued interest of her mother's relatives and friends.

No doubt they were concerned about her future. At twenty-seven, she was still unwed. There were suitors, of course. That same autumn it was rumoured that the French King wanted her for one of his noblemen, the following spring Queen Katherine was teasing her about the King of Poland's eagerness to marry her, and Duke Philip of Bavaria, who had been pursuing her intermittently for years, was still interested. Henry VIII, however, refrained from finding her a powerful husband. As the wife of an influential man, English or foreign, she could easily have become a rallying point for the Roman Catholics who opposed his policies, and an unmarried daughter was a useful pawn in his political manoeuvering, even if she was past her first youth.

Mary knew his opinion very well, and she once remarked that it was 'folly to think that they would marry me out of England or even in England, as long as my father lived . . . for I would be, while my father lived, only Lady Mary, the most unhappy lady in Christendom.' Had she still been Mary, Princess of Wales, it would have been a different matter, but her official illegitimacy made it unlikely that she would ever find a suitable husband.

She therefore continued her quiet, circumspect life, proudly signing herself 'Daughter of England', and emphasising her true rank by her rich costume, her jewellery and the lavishness of her household. In 1544, when she sat for her portrait, the artist depicted her as very much a royal lady. Her wavy, red-gold hair is neatly parted in the centre, her grey eyes are averted and her hands are clasped meekly before her, but her hood is set with rubies and pearls, a matching belt encircles her waist, a fine diamond pendant hangs from her pearl necklace, a ruby and diamond brooch is pinned to her bodice and there are rings on her fingers.

Her father augmented this rich collection of jewellery when she fell ill in the summer of 1546, and he made her two large gifts: diamond and ruby decorative bands for hoods, gem-set girdles, brooches with Biblical themes and a fine diamond cross. These adornments were not new. A diamond brooch in the form of the letters IHS (for Jesus) had once belonged to her friend, the Marchioness of Exeter, and Mary later gave it back to her. Another, set with a ruby above an emerald, a great pearl hanging beneath them, had on its back Catherine of Aragon's half-rose and pomegranate and had probably been hers. It is tempting to speculate that at least some of the other jewels had come from the same source. Was Henry, in a sentimental moment, trying to make amends to Mary for his past treatment of her before it was too late?

*Edward Seymour, Duke of Somerset,*
Lord Protector of England, by
M de Heere.
(Muncaster Castle: photograph,
Courtauld Institute of Art)

*Elizabeth*, aged about thirteen, by an unknown artist.
(The Royal Collection © 1993 Her Majesty The Queen)

*Edward VI and the Pope*, by an unknown artist, about 1548. Henry VIII is on his deathbed. To
the right of Edward VI are Somerset, probably Northumberland, of whom no other portrait is
known, and Cranmer.
(National Portrait Gallery, London)

The Choir, St George's Chapel, Windsor, where Henry VIII is buried.
(By courtesy of the Dean and Chapter of St George's Chapel: photograph, A F Kersting)

That year he suffered several near-fatal bouts of fever and at the end of December he drew up a new will. If he died, he would be succeeded by his son, Edward. Should Edward die childless, then Mary would succeed. If she too died without children, his younger daughter, Elizabeth, would become Queen. Almost immediately afterwards, he took a turn for the worse. Mary was at court, but neither she nor Queen Katherine was allowed into his bedchamber. Contrary to expectation he rallied, and was well enough to see the French and the imperial ambassadors on 16 January, but some days later he suffered another relapse. His doctors were privately forecasting his imminent demise, though they dared not say so to him and on 27 January, they sent for Thomas Cranmer, the Archbishop of Canterbury. He asked the King if he trusted in God. Beyond speech, Henry 'did wring his hand in his as hard as he could'. He died a few hours later and his nine-year-old son became King.

Edward VI was a solemn, grey-eyed boy, reserved and pious by nature. Mary was old enough to be his mother, but she had delighted in him from his earliest days, visiting him, making presents for him and asking about his progress. His Protestantism could have been a problem, but she had long since schooled herself to accept her father's Reformation, and in her innermost heart she cherished the hope that when Edward was older he would see the error of his ways and turn gladly to the Roman Catholic Church. The Emperor might mutter that the boy was the illegitimate child of an irregular union, but Mary accepted his accession without a qualm.

She had no desire to rule England. That was a task for a man, and although Edward was far too young to govern for himself, her father had foreseen that difficulty and had nominated a council of regency. One of its members was her old friend Sir Edward Seymour, now Earl of Hertford, the brother of Queen Jane. Henry had not singled him out for any special role, but as the young King's uncle he had an inestimable advantage and he grasped his opportunity. Before his fellow councillors could do anything about it, he had seized power, made himself Lord Protector of England and taken the title of Duke of Somerset.

A big, handsome, affable man with an approachable manner, he was hard-working and well-educated. He was also an austere Calvinist, but he had never made any public parade of his religion and Mary seems to have had no fears on that score. After all, it was not for him to change anything. He was simply holding the country in trust for her brother. She was slightly irritated when the Duke delayed coming to see her until several days after Henry's death, but she had no intention of falling out with him. She would, she told her friends, do whatever he suggested.

Of her actual feelings about Henry's demise, we have no hint. She spent the first few weeks afterwards with Queen Katherine, and she may have accompanied her to the funeral in St George's Chapel, Windsor, where her father was laid beside Queen Jane. Contemporary descriptions do not mention her presence, but there is no evidence of her being elsewhere. The first days of mourning over, she resumed her former way of life, while Edward occupied his King's apartments at Whitehall and Queen Katherine went to live at her Chelsea house, taking Elizabeth with her.

Mary was not shown her father's will, but that spring she gradually learned of its provisions. Most important was the recognition of her own position as heir to the throne. Her father had not restored her legitimacy, but by his orders she was now officially second person in the realm. He had also made her very wealthy, leaving to both his daughters lands providing each with an income of three thousand pounds a year, a considerable sum. Most of Mary's property lay in Essex, Suffolk and Norfolk, and it included not only the handsome manor of Hunsdon, where she had often stayed, but the mansion of Kenning-hall, formerly the property of the Duke of Norfolk, whom Henry had imprisoned, and her own favourite house of Beaulieu. With all this, she was now the fifth or sixth richest peer in England.

She travelled to East Anglia that summer, to view her new estates, and she set about appointing the necessary officials to administer them. Sir Robert Rochester, an Essex bachelor in his fifties, had already been running her financial affairs. She made him Controller of her household, and she recruited a number of other local gentlemen, including Henry Jerningham. Mary was popular in East Anglia, and she received an enthusiastic welcome wherever she went, but as the weeks slipped by she was becoming increasingly disturbed by reports from London.

First, there was the disquieting news about Katherine Parr. That April, less than three months after King Henry's death, she made a secret marriage with her old love, Thomas Seymour. Mary scarcely knew Thomas, for she had met him only once, but she had heard about his ruthless ambition, his jealousy of his brother, the Lord Protector, and his determination to find a royal bride. The Queen Dowager should never have lowered herself by marrying this adventurer. Mary did not go back to live at Chelsea after that, although her friendship with Katherine remained unimpaired and when the latter died of puerperal fever the following year, she left behind her an infant daughter whom she had named Mary.

Katherine's unsuitable marriage had been upsetting, but even more alarming were tales of the Lord Protector's religious alterations. There were stories of crosses and images being removed from churches, psalms being sung in English instead of Latin, and she heard too that Mass was no longer being said in the household of either the Lord Protector or his great rival Lord Dudley, now Earl of Warwick. Something would have to be done. Mary wrote an imperious letter to the Duke of Somerset, reminding him that her father had left the realm 'in godly order and quietness'. The Duke was upsetting everything with his unseemly innovations. At about the same time, her old friend Cardinal Reginald Pole dispatched a long letter to the Duke, condemning him for his 'pitch of extreme impiety'.

Somerset brushed aside the Cardinal's words as the outpourings of an unworldly fool, but he could not dismiss Mary's complaints so lightly. She was, after all, heir to the throne, and he had no desire to drive her into becoming leader of a Roman Catholic opposition. He therefore let it be known that he would not interfere with her religious practices as long as she acted discreetly. After all, she had accepted her father's Reformation, so why should she not acquiesce in his continuation of these policies?

In 1549 Archbishop Cranmer produced a Book of Common Prayer in English, and an Act of Uniformity ordered the fining or imprisonment of Roman Catholics who refused to attend the new form of service. Mary feared that the concept of sacrifice which lay at the heart of her faith would not be preserved, and she had heard that Protestants allowed the congregation to take the wine as well as the bread, instead of reserving it for the priest alone. To her, these were dreadful heresies and she was determined to oppose them.

As she rode about her estates, she did all she could to encourage the local priests to ignore the new form of service, and when the Act of Uniformity was passed she attended a particularly elaborate Mass in her chapel at Kenninghall. Formerly, she had gone to Mass twice a day. Now she went three times, and she invited all manner of strangers to come and worship with her attendants. Roman Catholic gentlemen began sending their daughters to her, to serve in her household, and one of these girls, Jane Dormer, became her favourite lady-in-waiting.

When the Privy Council wrote to rebuke her for breaking the law, she replied briskly that it was not she, but they, who were doing that. They had no business tampering with the ecclesiastical settlement during a royal minority. Her old ally Eustace Chapuys, the Emperor's ambassador, had long since retired, but one day she was fortunate enough to find herself standing next to his successor, Francis van der Delft, at the christening of Lady Warwick's latest child. During a lengthy interval in the proceedings, she engaged him in animated conversation, addressing him in several different languages and impressing him with her fluency. She followed up this encounter by plying him with frequent letters and invitations, and when he went to see her she was almost embarrassingly grateful. Soon, he was deeply involved in trying to help her.

The Emperor's own attitude was rather less vigorous than she could have wished. She had better avoid antagonising the Lord Protector, he said, and even if she were deprived of the Mass she should not protest, for there would

*Thomas Cranmer, Archbishop of Canterbury*, by Gerlach Flicke, 1546.
(National Portrait Gallery, London)

*Anne Stanhope, Duchess of Somerset*, the Lord Protector's unpopular wife, by an unknown artist.
(National Gallery of Ireland, Dublin)

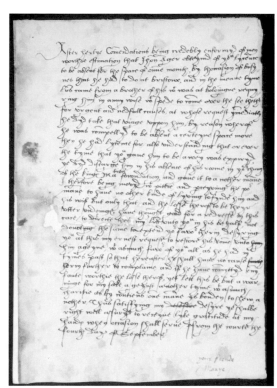

Letter from Mary to the Dean and Chapter of Westminster, on behalf of a bedesman, signed 'Your friend Mary', before 1553. (By courtesy of the Dean and Chapter of Westminster)

Clock in the form of a nef, believed to have belonged to Charles V. (Musée Nationale de la Renaissance, Ecouen: © Photo RMN)

be no stain on her conscience were she forcibly prevented from attending. That was not the attitude Mary had in mind, and she persisted in her pleas until Charles V instructed Van der Delft to ask Somerset for letters patent protecting her right to worship as she pleased in the privacy of her own household. The letters were never issued, but Van der Delft did manage to extract a spoken promise from Somerset, or thought he had, and with that she appeared to be satisfied.

The Lord Protector was, in fact, in grave difficulties. In 1549 Roman Catholics in Devon and Cornwall rose in revolt against his religious innovations, and the peasants of Norfolk rebelled against the government's land enclosure policy. Even more dangerously, his own fellow peers were tired of him. He was indecisive, he was snappish, he could not delegate, he ignored their advice, he did not live in the lavish manner appropriate to his high office and, most annoyingly of all, he appeared to be ruled by his unpleasant wife. By the autumn of that year, they were plotting against him.

The Earl of Warwick, his old rival, was leader of the conspiracy, a handsome, energetic man much admired for the magnificence of his lifestyle and his military prowess. He now approached Mary, asking her to approve his plans to overthrow the Lord Protector. Rumour had it that he meant to make her Regent and then restore the old religion, but she did not believe a word of it. Envy and greed were the conspirators' true motives, she said. 'The Earl of Warwick is the most unstable man in England,' she told Van der Delft. 'You will see that no good will come of this move, but that it is a punishment from heaven and may be only the beginning of our misfortunes.'

Shrugging off her lack of interest, Warwick went ahead with his plans, and a few weeks later he had the Lord Protector arrested on a charge of treason while he himself took possession of the startled young King. When she heard the news, Mary was overcome with dread. She might not have agreed with Somerset's policies, but she did not believe that he would ever have harmed her. Warwick was very different. He did eventually release Somerset from his imprisonment, but the former Lord Protector's power was at an end and there was no knowing when Warwick might turn against him again. He was not safe and neither was Mary. Reviving a previous notion, she told Van der Delft that he must help her to escape to the safety of the Low Countries.

The ambassador obediently wrote to Charles V, but as usual the Emperor had no desire for his cousin to come to his court. If she left England, he pointed out, she would be throwing away any chance of inheriting the throne should something happen to Edward. Were her brother to die when she was out of the country, those in power would undoubtedly turn to the next in line after her: the Protestant Elizabeth. Mary should stay where she was.

She thought otherwise. 'If my brother were to die,' she wrote to Van der Delft, 'I should be far better out of the kingdom, because as soon as he were dead, before the public knew it, they would dispatch me too. There is no doubt of that, because you know that there is nobody about the King's person or in the government who is not inimical to me.' She bullied the ambassador, pleaded with the Emperor, and finally convinced him that her life was in grave danger. Much perturbed, he agreed to send ships to rescue her, and he told his sister, the Queen Dowager, to arrange it.

Van der Delft had recently been given permission to return to Brussels because he was suffering from a serious illness, but he felt responsible for Mary. As he said himself, she seemed to cling to him, and so he promised to come back for her in person. He set sail for the Low Countries, but by the time he arrived he was so ill that he had to take to his bed. There he lay, raving in delirium about ships and secret meetings and ladies in distress. When reports reached the Queen Dowager's ears, she was strongly tempted to cancel the whole enterprise for fear that he had unwittingly revealed everything.

The ambassador did not recover. He died on 21 June, but Charles urged his sister to go ahead with her plans in order to save their cousin. Accordingly, a small flotilla of warships set off towards Harwich at the end of the month, on the pretext of chasing a notorious Scottish pirate from the North Sea. On board one of the vessels was Van der Delft's secretary, Jean Dubois, whom Mary had often met in the ambassador's company. It now fell to him to lead the expedition.

Mary was staying at Woodham Walter in Essex when word came that Dubois had arrived in the nearby port of Maldon, disguised as a corn merchant. He was ready to take her away, he said, and was awaiting her instructions. When she read his message, she was immediately thrown into a panic. It had been all very well to dream of escape, to imagine herself sailing away, leaving all her troubles behind her, but now that the moment had come she was overwhelmed by doubts. How could she bear to leave all her friends and live among strangers? She would be abandoning those faithful Roman Catholics who looked to her for leadership. She could not possibly go, and yet how could she stay, now that the Emperor had sent his ships for her?

In an agony of indecision, she began packing her belongings into long hopsacks, while her Controller, Sir Robert Rochester, went to fetch Dubois. Perhaps she could delay, plead for time and say she was not ready. When Dubois was admitted to her presence, she had scarcely completed the usual civilities of asking about the health of the Emperor and the Queen Dowager before she blurted out, 'I do not know how the Emperor would take it if it turned out to be impossible to go now, after I have so often importuned his Majesty on the subject!'

Having spent the past few hours listening to Sir Robert pouring out all the many reasons why his mistress should not leave the country, Dubois was not altogether surprised. He replied soothingly that as long as Mary was satisfied, Charles V would be content. If she did not wish to go now, Dubois could slip

*A View of Maldon*, engraved in 1832 by J C Armytage after G B Campion. (Reproduced by courtesy of Essex Record Office)

away as he had come, and no harm would be done. If she did mean to go, however, speed was essential.

More distraught than ever, Mary began to speak agitatedly about her rings, the hopsacks and her other belongings. Perhaps they would get lost on the way to Brussels. She must not worry about that, said Dubois. She would find everything she needed there. Still undecided, she turned anxiously to confer with Sir Robert and her principal lady, Mrs Clarentius. After a lengthy confabulation, she finally announced that she would be ready to go; not that day or the next, but the day after that.

Even as she spoke, there was a loud hammering at the door and Sir Robert hurried out to speak to the visitor, a local man. He came back with a face of doom. Dubois was liable to be arrested at any moment, he said. His boat might be seized. Guards had been posted in the church tower. Moreover, his informant had told him that there was 'something mysterious in the air'. 'What shall we do?' cried Mary in despair. 'What is to become of me?' and she repeated these words helplessly, over and over again.

Since she seemed incapable of deciding anything, Sir Robert hastily told Dubois that they would send for him when they were ready, and in exasperation the secretary prepared to leave. Guided by one of Rochester's friends, he got safely to his little boat, and as it sailed out of Maldon Harbour he looked back at the church tower to see if anyone was watching. There was no one there, and he felt sure that Sir Robert's warnings had been deliberately designed to put an end to the enterprise. Whatever she might have said before, Mary obviously did not want to go. There was no point in trying again. Come what might, she was obviously resolved to stay in England.

Reports of the mysterious visitor soon reached the Privy Council in London, and they decided that Mary must be moved away from the coast as quickly as possible, in case the Emperor tried again to take her away. Lord Chancellor Rich was sent down to Essex to suggest that she come to court, but she dared not comply. Once in London, there was no knowing what might happen. She would be at Warwick's mercy. She was unwell, she said, unfit to travel. Rich

*Richard, 1st Baron Rich*, Lord Chancellor of England, by Holbein.
(The Royal Collection © 1993 Her Majesty The Queen)

*Elizabeth Jenks, Lady Rich*, the Lord
Chancellor's wife and mother of his
fifteen children, by Holbein.
(The Royal Collection © 1993
Her Majesty The Queen)

*Edward VI* at the age of nine, by William
Scrots, 1546.
(National Portrait Gallery, London)

retreated, but a few days later he was back again, this time accompanied by his
wife. Would Lady Mary care to visit their estates, they asked. There was
excellent hunting to be had, and the change of air would do her good. Once
more, she refused.

A long and argumentative correspondence with Warwick ensued, Mary
insisting that she had received permission to worship as she chose, he
denying knowledge of any such concession. When Van der Delft's successor
Jehan Scheyfre urged her to moderate her tone, she retorted that she was in the
habit of writing 'roughly' to the council, and if she adopted a milder manner
they might think that they had won her over. At the end of January 1551,
however, she was considerably shaken to receive a letter signed by the King
himself. It rebuked her for her recent behaviour, and told her that she had
never been promised freedom of worship. Her position as Edward's sister
made her offence all the graver, it went on, for she was setting a bad example
to the rest of his subjects.

She thought at first that this was simply another of Warwick's missives with
the King's signature appended, but then she saw that the last paragraph was
in Edward's own writing. Not only did he summarise the main points, but he
ended, 'I will see my laws strictly obeyed, and those who break them shall be
watched and denounced.' She was aghast. Her beloved little brother had
somehow turned into a cold stranger. His words, she told him when she wrote
back, 'have caused me more suffering than any illness, even unto death'. He
had obviously been misled by vindictive councillors and, intelligent though
he was beyond others of his age, he should suspend judgment on spiritual
matters until he reached 'ripe and fuller years'.

To make matters worse, she heard that Elizabeth was very much in favour
with Warwick. She and Edward had been seen at a bull-baiting with the Duke

and the French ambassador, chatting so animatedly together that they seemed to be paying no attention to the sport. What could it mean? Despite her misgivings, Mary decided to go to London to see for herself.

No lavish welcome awaited her when she rode up with four hundred gentlemen and her own attendants. The Controller of the King's Household, Sir Antony Wingfield, came out alone to meet her and took her into a gallery where Edward VI stood, flanked by more than two dozen Privy Councillors. Mary knelt to him, explaining that illness had prevented her from coming sooner. He remarked with irritating self-satisfaction that God had sent her sickness while granting him health. He then led her into his own chamber. The Privy Councillors trooped in after them, but Mary's ladies-in-waiting were forced to remain outside.

A small, proud figure, she stood amidst the tall, sumptuously clad men and determinedly defended herself as they accused her of breaking the laws of the kingdom by adhering to the old religion. She had been promised freedom of worship, she said over and over again, but they denied it, and in the end she turned to the King, urging him to defer any decision until he was older and had greater understanding. He was, after all, not yet fourteen. Stung by what he considered to be her patronising manner, he retorted that she might also yet have something to learn, for 'no one was too old for that'.

His councillors hastily intervened but, in the face of Mary's repeated assertion that the current policy was not of her brother's making but was their doing, Warwick, too, lost his temper and snarled at her, 'How now, My Lady? It seems that Your Grace is trying to show us in a hateful light to the King our master, without any cause whatsoever!' She could not hide the truth, she cried. She was doing her best to comply, and although her soul was God's, she offered her body to the King's service and would rather Edward took away her life than deprived her of the old religion.

Shocked by that, and by her haggard appearance, the boy hastened to assure her that he wished for no such sacrifice. He allowed her to go back to her lodgings while his councillors conferred together anxiously. What was to be done about her obstinacy? Much as they might have liked to send her to the Tower, they dared not risk bringing down the wrath of the Emperor. In the end, they agreed to turn a blind eye to her disobedience, at least for the time being. The following day, Secretary Petre visited her and found her ill in bed. Edward had been distressed at her condition, he said, and did not wish to worry her. She could return to her estates whenever she pleased. A few days later, she left London.

This truce lasted for several months but in August the council decided that they could 'wink at sin no longer'. Summoning Mary herself was no use, they knew, and so they tackled Sir Robert Rochester and two of her other gentlemen, Sir Francis Englefield and Edward Walgrave, telling them that they must abolish the Mass in her household. Horrified, they said that their mistress would never permit it. They did try to pass on a modified version of the council's message, but when Mary flatly refused to listen, they said that they dared not approach her again about it. They were thereupon arrested, and yet another deputation rode down to see her, this time at Copped Hall in Essex.

Lord Chancellor Rich was accompanied by Sir William Petre and Sir Anthony Wingfield. Mary had them shown into her presence, and when they produced a letter from Edward she fell to her knees, saying that she would kiss

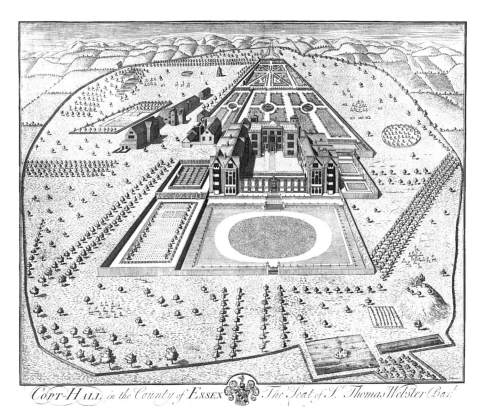

Copped Hall, Essex.
(Reproduced by courtesy of Essex Record Office)

the package not for its contents, but because it came from the King. In front of her entire household she opened it and read the letter, exclaiming aloud, 'Ah! Good Master Cecil took much pain here!' Still convinced that her brother had no part in her persecution, she was sure that the author of this particular missive was William Cecil, the Principal Secretary and a noted Protestant.

Lord Chancellor Rich then began to speak, but she interrupted him, telling him to be brief, for she was unwell. She was not to have the Mass or any other illegal service, he declared, but when he tried to list the names of the councillors who had given this order, she cut him short again, saying that she had no need to hear who they were, 'for I know you to be all of one sort therein'. None of her chaplains was to be allowed to say Mass, he went on, and none of her servants was to hear it. Rather than hear any service other than that used at the time of her father's death, she exclaimed, she would lay her head on the block and suffer death.

They could prevent her priests from saying Mass and her servants from attending, but 'no new service shall be used in my house, and if any be said in it, I will not tarry in the house'. She reminded them, too, that she had Charles V's protection, adding contemptuously. 'Though you esteem little the Emperor, yet should you show more favour to me, for my father's sake, who made the most part of you almost [from] nothing!'

The thought of her own imprisoned gentlemen gave her courage, and she angrily brushed aside Rich's offer to send her a replacement for Sir Robert Rochester. She would appoint her own officers, and if they sent her men she

would leave at once, for she would not live in the same house as any of them.
'And (quoth she)', Lord Rich reported, ' "I am sickly and yet I will not die
willingly, but will do the best I can to preserve my life; but if I shall chance to
die I will protest openly that you of the council be the cause of my death. You
give me fair words, but your deeds be always ill towards me."'

She ended the interview by fetching a ring, which she handed, kneeling, to
the Lord Chancellor. It was for the King, a token that she would die his true
subject and sister, obeying his commandments in all things save in matters
touching the Mass and the new service. So saying she rose, turned on her heel
and strode out, leaving them disconcerted.

Trying to regain the initiative, they summoned her chaplains and the rest of
her servants, making them promise not to attend any more services according
to the old religion, but Mary was determined to have the last word. As they left
the house she appeared at an upstairs window to harangue them further. She
wanted her Controller back as soon as possible, she called out imperiously.
Since his departure she had been forced to keep her own accounts, 'and learn
how many loaves of bread be made of a bushel of wheat: and this my father
and my mother never brought me up with baking and brewing, and to be
plain with you, I am weary with my office.'

As soon as they arrived back in London, Rich and his fellow councillors sent
Rochester, Englefield and Walgrave to the Tower, and there they stayed until
the following March. Mary, for her part, told most of her chaplains that they
must leave her for their own protection, but she continued to hear Mass
secretly, ignoring the warnings of the Emperor and the Queen Dowager. They
knew only too well that Warwick was fiercely ambitious. He had recently
taken the title of Duke of Northumberland, and he would not let anyone stand
in his way. Indeed that October he had the Duke of Somerset arrested once
more, this time on a charge of plotting to murder him. The former Lord
Protector was tried, found guilty of treason and sentenced to death. He was
executed on 22 January 1552, still protesting his innocence.

# 5

## QUEEN JANE

*E*WARD HAD ALWAYS been a healthy child, but towards the end of 1552 he fell ill, and with every passing week he was worse. He suffered from bouts of high fever with a dreadful cough. He grew thin, pale and exhausted. He could not eat, his body swelled and he began to spit blood. Like his half-brother, the Duke of Richmond, he had probably contracted tuberculosis. His doctors tried every treatment they knew, but nothing did any good and those closest to him realised that he was dying.

The Duke of Northumberland began to cultivate Lady Mary. Suddenly, he was sending her all the latest news from court, granting her money to repair her properties, urging her to use the coat of arms she had borne as Princess of Wales. When she went to see Edward early in 1553, the Duke's eldest son rode out to meet her with a hundred horsemen. She arrived at the outer gate of the palace to find Northumberland himself waiting to welcome her, with all the Privy Council. He spoke to her respectfully, almost as though she were already Queen, but she did not trust him.

*Lady Jane Grey*, attributed to Master John, about 1545.
(National Portrait Gallery, London)

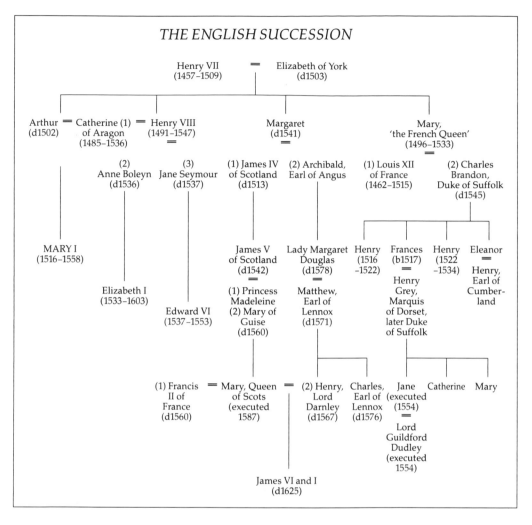

# THE ENGLISH SUCCESSION

Henry VII (1457–1509) = Elizabeth of York (d1503)

Arthur (d1502) = Catherine (1) of Aragon (1485–1536) = Henry VIII (1491–1547)

Margaret (d1541)

Mary, 'the French Queen' (1496–1533)

(2) Anne Boleyn (d1536)    (3) Jane Seymour (d1537)

(1) James IV of Scotland (d1513)    (2) Archibald, Earl of Angus

(1) Louis XII of France (1462–1515)    (2) Charles Brandon, Duke of Suffolk (d1545)

MARY I (1516–1558)

James V of Scotland (d1542)    Lady Margaret Douglas (d1578)    Henry (1516–1522)    Frances (b1517) = Henry Grey, Marquis of Dorset, later Duke of Suffolk    Henry (1522–1534)    Eleanor = Henry, Earl of Cumberland

Elizabeth I (1533–1603)

Edward VI (1537–1553)

(1) Princess Madeleine (2) Mary of Guise (d1560)    Matthew, Earl of Lennox (d1571)

(1) Francis II of France (d1560) = Mary, Queen of Scots (executed 1587) = (2) Henry, Lord Darnley (d1567)    Charles, Earl of Lennox (d1576)    Jane (executed 1554) = Lord Guildford Dudley (executed 1554)    Catherine    Mary

James VI and I (d1625)

---

Although Edward was confined to his bedchamber, he seemed glad to see her and spoke pleasantly, of uncontroversial matters, making no mention of religion. After she had left court, however, and his condition deteriorated still further, he became increasingly preoccupied with the problem of what would happen were he to die. Fervent Protestant that he was, he could not contemplate leaving his kingdom to his devout Roman Catholic sister. The Duke of Northumberland was even more worried, for a different reason. His attempts to ingratiate himself with Mary had failed. He realised that if she came to the throne, he would instantly lose his position of pre-eminence. She would avenge herself on her enemies, and he would find himself in the Tower. He and the King had long discussions about the succession, and between them they devised a solution. They would ignore Henry VIII's will, which had the force of law. They would not allow either Mary or Elizabeth to succeed, on the grounds that they were illegitimate. Instead, Edward would bequeath his throne to as good a Protestant as himself: Lady Jane Grey.

Jane had been born and brought up in the country at Bradgate Park, her parents' home in Leicestershire. The eldest of three sisters, she was a clever, scholarly girl. Her indecisive father, the Duke of Suffolk, was ruled by her domineering Protestant mother, Mary and Edward's cousin, Frances. Jane once told Roger Ascham, the Cambridge scholar, that her parents always treated her severely. She sought solace in her studies, for John Aylmer, her tutor, was kind to her, and together they read Latin, Greek, Hebrew, French and Italian.

When she was ten, Thomas Seymour hatched a plot to marry her to the young King, his nephew, so that he could rule England on their behalf. The scheme fell through and Thomas eventually went to the block for his treasonable activities, but Jane had come to everyone's attention as a possible bride for Edward. No one knows whether it was Edward himself or the Duke of Northumberland who devised the new plan, but the King called his statesmen to his bedchamber one by one and his condition was so pitiful that they did not have the heart to deny him his wish. Lady Jane would become Queen of England when he died. That settled, the Duke of Northumberland promptly married her to his youngest son, Lord Guildford Dudley.

Mary knew Lady Jane. She had even made her a present of one of her own pearl necklaces. 'Given to my cousin Jane Grey', says a later annotation in the margin of the 1547 inventory of her jewels. She knew her and she did not think her of much account, but she realised now that the girl was part of a sinister plot. The Duke of Northumberland had tried to keep the seriousness of the King's condition from Mary, but the Emperor's ambassador made sure that she was aware of the latest news and she must have held desperate discussions with Sir Robert Rochester, Mrs Clarentius and the other members of her household. There must have been those who urged her to flee there and then, but there were others who told her that, if she did leave, the throne would never be hers. She decided to stay.

Fearing for her future, Charles V dispatched three special ambassadors to England, ostensibly to enquire about Edward's health but really to do what they could to save Mary's life. By then, the boy was sinking fast and the Duke of Northumberland summoned Mary and Elizabeth to their brother's deathbed. Forewarned, they did not go. Elizabeth set out, but turned back, and Mary stayed at Hunsdon. On 6 July 1553, the day that Charles's ambassadors arrived in London, Edward died.

Less than twenty-four hours later, Northumberland had Jane brought to his magnificent mansion at Syon, and there he broke the news to her that she was Queen. He and the Privy Council then held a lavish banquet to celebrate. Jane hated the Duke, disliked her pretty, fair-haired husband and had no desire to rule England, but she had to obey. The following afternoon, in bright sunshine, she was taken by barge to the Tower of London, where she would spend the traditional days before her coronation.

Wearing a green and gold dress and a jewelled hood, she walked in procession through the gates and up into the Great Hall of the Tower. Her noblemen bore a canopy of state over her head, and her mother marched behind her, triumphantly carrying her train. His chosen monarch safely in his hands, the Duke of Northumberland turned his attention to Mary. He had heard that she had fled to East Anglia and, summoning three of his sons, Warwick, Lord Robert and Lord Ambrose, Northumberland went out to hunt her down.

When Mary heard that the King was on the point of death, she rode by night to Cambridgeshire, arriving after a difficult and dangerous journey at Sawston Hall. The next night, she moved on to Euston Hall, near Thetford, where her widowed friend, Lady Burgh, lived. There, one of her London goldsmiths,

The Tower of London. (Photograph, Clive Friend)

*Lord Robert Dudley*, Northumberland's son, later Earl of Leicester, about 1560, by Steven van der Meulen. (Reproduced by permission of the Trustees of the Wallace Collection)

*Opposite*. Framlingham Castle, Suffolk, where Mary's forces assembled. (English Heritage)

Kenninghall, Norfolk. The windows are from the mansion which belonged to Mary. (Reproduced by permission of His Grace the Duke of Norfolk)

Robert Raynes, came with the news she was expecting. Her brother was dead. She did not dare believe him in case it was a trap. If Northumberland tricked her into declaring herself Queen while Edward was still alive, she would be guilty of treason. She must have confirmation of the news. Saying nothing, she hurried on to her own house at Kenninghall in Norfolk. Almost at once, Dr Thomas Hughes arrived to assure her that the report was true. King Edward was dead. Summoning all her servants, Mary declared herself Queen and her household cheered excitedly. She then sent one of her men, Thomas Hungate, to the Duke of Northumberland, ordering him to issue proclamations throughout the country announcing her accession. Thomas bravely delivered his message, and was promptly thrown into the Tower.

Her letters to the gentlemen of East Anglia met with a better reception, and within hours they were rallying to her cause. First to arrive were Sir Henry Bedingfeld at Oxburgh Hall and his two brothers, then Sir Richard Southwell came, a particularly welcome addition. The wealthiest knight in Norfolk, he brought supplies of men and money as well as provisions. Soon others were flocking to Kenninghall, and not merely from the local area. The Earl of Bath had already given Mary his allegiance and the Earl of Sussex was among the early arrivals.

Realising that her present residence was neither large enough nor well enough fortified, Mary decided to move to Framlingham Castle in Suffolk.

*Thomas Radcliffe, 3rd Earl of Sussex*, by an unknown artist, after a painting of about 1565.
(National Portrait Gallery, London)

*Sir Richard Southwell*, the richest knight in Norfolk, by Holbein.
(The Royal Collection © 1993 Her Majesty The Queen)

*Thomas, 2nd Baron Wentworth*, 1568, attributed to Van der Meulen.
(National Portrait Gallery, London)

*Sir Henry Bedingfeld*, one of Mary's first supporters, by an unknown artist. (The National Trust, at Oxburgh Hall: Henry Bedingfeld)

When she rode up at about eight o'clock on the evening of 12 July, she found the deer park below the castle crowded with local gentlemen, justices of the peace and ordinary country people come to lend their support. The Earl of Sussex had gone away to fetch his forces and he now came back with an impressive array of both cavalry and infantry. The Earl of Bath also brought a large contingent of men. The situation was looking more hopeful by the hour, and that night word came that the crews of five royal ships searching for Mary had mutinied in her favour.

By 16 July, more noblemen and more soldiers had arrived. Thomas, Lord Wentworth, had originally pledged his loyalty to Jane, but a message from Mary persuaded him to change his mind and when he rode up to Framlingham, in an especially splendid suit of armour, everyone was much impressed and morale rose higher still. Mary made him second in command to her general, the Earl of Sussex. Sir Henry Bedingfeld became Knight Marshal, and together these experienced men began drilling the soldiers and organising the army. Not a moment was to be lost, for the Duke of Northumberland and his forces were fast approaching.

When she heard that the Duke was less than thirty miles away, near Bury St Edmunds, Mary ordered her army to muster and stand ready to meet the enemy. Once they were drawn up in battle order, she announced that she would inspect them. It was four in the afternoon on 20 July when she rode from the castle on her white horse. Seeing the lines of armed men, her mount reared nervously and she had to order some of the foot-soldiers to lift her down from the saddle. Telling her general that no gun or arrow was to be fired until she had completed her inspection, she went round the infantry on foot, speaking in an easy and friendly way to the men, with no hint of nervousness or strain in her manner.

When she had inspected the foot-soldiers, she remounted, to watch a large detachment of cavalry thunder across one of the fields. Delighted by the spectacle, she spent at least three hours with her forces. The enemy might be near at hand, but she was becoming more and more confident. Reports were coming in from all over the country of huge crowds rising to support her, and she may already have heard that Northumberland was in difficulties.

Instead of fighting for him, the people of Suffolk were hurrying to join Mary. Savagely angry, he turned back towards Cambridge, burning the houses of the local landowners who supported her. That alienated his companions. Lord Clinton, James Crofts and others deserted him and sought Mary's pardon. The Earl of Oxford, Lord Grey of Wilton and Lord Rich followed. Seeing their leaders disappearing, the Duke's ordinary soldiers melted away.

In London, the Privy Council decided that they had made a terrible mistake. Mary was obviously the true Queen, not Jane. On their orders, the Lord Mayor of London proclaimed her at Cheapside, to tumultuous cheers. 'All the people and citizens of London for so joyful news made great and many fires through all the streets and lanes within the said city,' one Londoner reported, 'with setting tables in the streets and banqueting also, with all the bells ringing in every parish church in London until ten of the clock at night.' An Italian resident was equally impressed. 'Men ran hither and thither,' he told a friend, 'bonnets flew into the air, shouts rose higher than the stars, fires were lit on all sides and all the bells were set a-pealing, and from a distance the earth must have looked like a Mount Etna.'

*William, 1st Lord Paget of Beaudesert*, by an unknown artist.
(The National Trust, at Plas Newydd: photograph, Courtauld Institute of Art)

The Wingfield Room from Wingfield House, where Mary stayed, and now in Christchurch Mansion, Ipswich.
(Ipswich Borough Council Museums and Galleries)

As soon as the proclamation at Cheapside was over, the Earl of Arundel and Lord Paget rode for Framlingham with the Great Seal. Meanwhile, the Duke of Suffolk read out the proclamation on Tower Hill, then went back into the Council Chamber in the Tower to find his daughter, Jane, sitting alone beneath her canopy of state. He tore the canopy down with his own hands, and told her that she would no longer need it. He offered no further explanation, and it was left to her attendants to tell her that she was no longer Queen. She had always known it, she said. The Crown had never been hers. It belonged to Mary. When she saw her father again, she asked him if she could go home. She could not, he replied. They were both prisoners.

Back in Cambridge once more, the Duke of Northumberland realised that all was lost. When he heard that the Privy Council had changed sides, he ordered his secretary to fill his bonnet with gold coins, summoned a herald and strode out into the market square. He listened impassively as the herald proclaimed Mary as Queen, and then he threw his bonnet up into the air, shouting out three times over, 'God save Queen Mary!' The coins fell to the ground and the onlookers scrambled after them, but it was too late for the Duke to change sides now. The Mayor of Cambridge had him arrested and a day or two later the Earl of Arundel, Lord Grey and Henry Jerningham arrived to take charge of him.

When they entered his apartment, the Duke fell to his knees, begging Arundel to be good to him.

'And consider,' he wailed, 'I have done nothing but by the consent of you and all the whole Council!'

'My Lord', replied Arundel, 'I am sent hither by the Queen's Majesty, and in her name I do arrest you.'

'And I obey it, My Lord,' cried Northumberland eagerly, 'and I beseech you, My Lord of Arundel, use mercy towards me, knowing the case as it is.'

*Henry, 12th Earl of Arundel*, by an artist of the studio of Van der Meulen.
(National Portrait Gallery, London)

'My Lord,' replied Arundel sternly, 'You should have sought for mercy sooner. I must do according to my commandments.'

Putting on his scarlet cloak, Northumberland mounted his horse and rode in the rain with his captors to London. Through jeering crowds they went to the Tower of London, amidst cries of 'Traitor!' The Duke was soon joined by the three sons who had gone with him to East Anglia, and by the Marquis of Northampton and the Earl of Huntingdon. Their remaining forces fled, and their horses were seized for the new Queen's service.

Mary, at Framlingham, was at the centre of exhausting, exhilarating activity. Now that the danger was receding, the hundreds of men who had flocked to her could be sent home again, but dozens of Northumberland's former supporters were hurrying to seek her pardon. Most she received graciously but a few she rebuffed. Bishop Ridley, for instance, had not only usurped Thomas Bonner's position as Bishop of London, but had publicly preached against her just a few days before. Far from accepting his protestations of loyalty, she sent him to the Tower.

More Privy Councillors were also arriving from London with expressions of apology and regret. She forgave them, but when she attended their meetings she was astonished. There were deep divisions within the council, 'whose members were accusing one another, trying to disculpate themselves, chopping and changing in such a manner' that she was unable to get at the truth of what had happened, she told one of the imperial ambassadors afterwards. When she asked when she ought to move to the capital, they all gave different advice. Some said she should wait because of the hot weather, the bad air and the danger of plague in the city, but others urged her to press on so that she could put affairs in order and establish herself securely.

There was so much business to transact that she hardly knew where to begin. She had never attended council meetings before, or read state papers. She was told that she must renew all her ambassadors' commissions, but before she could give her mind to that, reports came in suggesting that the French might take this opportunity to attack Calais, which belonged to England. She was thrown into a panic at the news, and the Deputy Governor's assurance that he would do his best to defend the city 'like a gentleman and a man of honour' was not much consolation.

She did not trust any of her councillors, but Lord Paget with his round, bland face, his forked beard and his shrewd glance was always at her elbow, offering practical advice and telling her how devoted he was to the Emperor. Probably at his urging, she decided to set off for London as soon as possible and, accompanied by a guard of several hundred men and a long procession of supporters, she left Framlingham on 24 July. Her first stop was at Ipswich, where the bailiffs met her on the heath above the town and made her a gift of eleven pounds sterling in gold. As she rode through the streets she paused so that some pretty little boys could give her a golden heart inscribed with the words, 'the heart of the people'. She lodged that night in Wingfield House, hoping for a few days' rest and quiet, but the stream of recently hostile but now contrite visitors continued; the Duchess of Richmond, widow of her illegitimate brother, Sir William Cecil and his brother-in-law, Nicholas Bacon, among the rest.

Two days later she left for Colchester, to stay with Muriel Christmas, one of her mother's old servants, and then she sought the seclusion of her favourite residence, Beaulieu. Still the visitors came. Gertrude, Marchioness of Exeter, released at last from the Tower, arrived for a joyful reunion. The Duchess of Suffolk rode up at two o'clock in the morning, dishevelled and distraught, begging for the lives of her husband and her daughter, Jane. Mary listened to her sympathetically and made promises. She had no intention of executing either of them.

They would have to stay where they were for the time being, of course, but she would not harm them. Less successful was the Duchess of Northumberland. As she approached Beaulieu, Mary's servants stopped her, saying that the Queen did not wish to speak to her. The imperial ambassadors saw her

*Anne Cooke, Lady Bacon,* one of Mary's chamberwomen, a painted terracotta bust.
(Private collection: photograph, Courtauld Institute of Art)

riding disconsolately back to London as they arrived to present the Emperor's congratulations.

Mary was overjoyed to see them, and when the formal audience was over she asked them to send one of their number to speak to her privately. Simon Renard, an ambitious, highly-strung lawyer from the Franche-Comté was chosen, and he made his way in through a back door to her oratory that evening. A former ambassador to France and something of a protégé of the Queen Dowager, he was about Mary's own age. They took to each other at once, and soon he was passing on the Emperor's advice with sympathy and tact.

Charles V had been delighted when he had heard Mary's news, but he had warned that she must 'take very great care, at the outset, not to be led by her zeal to be too hasty in reforming matters that may not seem to be proceeding in a right manner, but to show herself to be accommodating'. She would have to reassure those who remembered that she was half-Spanish by birth and suspected that she was wholly Spanish in outlook. Moreover, she must not antagonise her Privy Councillors by giving them the impression that she intended to rule alone, without their advice.

Mary received these comments with composure, but she remarked with alarming ingenuousness that they, her councillors, knew her to be a Roman Catholic. They were perfectly well aware that she had been hearing Mass secretly for months, and they would not be in the least surprised when she reintroduced it generally. She could do no less, she said, for she must not be thankless for the favour shown her by God in choosing her, His unworthy servant, for this lofty position.

She then dismayed him still further by announcing that she meant to give her brother a Roman Catholic funeral. That would alienate many of her people, he warned. She answered that her conscience would not permit her to do anything else, and he saw that her remark that 'she felt so strongly on the matter of religion that she was hardly to be moved' was nothing less than the truth. Eventually he persuaded her to abandon the idea, but he feared that there could be grave difficulties ahead.

Soon after their interview, she left for London, calling at Sir William Petre's house at Ingatestone, then moving on towards Havering. All along the way, crowds came out to cheer her. Everyone was delighted with her. She might be small and thin, with a sadly careworn countenance, but she was King Harry's daughter.

As she approached the outskirts of the capital, she found another procession coming towards her. Elizabeth was riding out to welcome her. Elizabeth had already sent congratulations, and a polite letter asking if she should wear mourning. Now, she knelt before Mary, and the assembled courtiers held their breath. How would Catherine of Aragon's daughter greet Anne Boleyn's child? The two had probably not seen each other for several years, and Elizabeth was now a tall, thin redhead of nineteen. In that moment of emotion, when everything Mary had hoped for seemed to be coming true, she raised her half-sister, embraced her with a warm smile and kissed her. Turning to Elizabeth's ladies-in-waiting, she embraced each of them in a singular mark of favour. She then indicated that Elizabeth was to ride in the place of honour, immediately behind herself. It seemed that she was ready to forget the past.

Preceded by the Earl of Arundel bearing the sword of state, Queen Mary rode into her capital city. She had changed into a dress of purple satin and

Panel in the Beauchamp Tower, Tower of London, carved by or for the Duke of Northumberland's son, John, while he and his brothers were imprisoned there. (Collections/Bartholomew)

velvet, the skirt and sleeves heavily embroidered with gold. On her head she wore a hood studded with dazzling jewels. The Lord Mayor greeted her, bells pealed, guns fired thunderous salutes and the crowds surged forward with deafening cheers.

When she finally reached the Tower of London she saw before her, kneeling on the grass, a pathetic little group of familiar figures. Stephen Gardiner, Bishop of Winchester, had been held prisoner there for the past five years for his opposition to the Protestant innovations. The old Duke of Norfolk had been there for even longer, incarcerated by Henry VIII on a charge of treason. Finally, there was the handsome young son of the Marchioness of Exeter. The captives held up their hands in mute supplication. Weeping, Mary hurried over to them and raised each one of them, embracing them and kissing them. 'You are my prisoners now,' she said, when she could speak, and she led them into the royal apartments.

The Duke of Northumberland was tried before his peers in Westminster Hall on 18 August 1553. Mary was not there, but the Duke of Norfolk presided. Restored to his old position of Earl Marshal, he sat on a high platform, in front of a rich cloth of state. Northumberland's confession was read out, he knelt to beg for mercy, but Norfolk condemned him to death and he was taken back to the Tower. He was executed on 22 August.

Two of his fellow conspirators died with him, but they were the only others to suffer the death penalty. Mary had no bloodthirsty taste for vengeance. Lady Jane and her husband were tried and found guilty of treason, but she flatly refused to execute them, saying that the girl had done no wrong. Northumberland's other three sons, who had ridden to Cambridgeshire with him, likewise escaped execution, although they too had to remain in the Tower for the time being. At least one of these boys was probably Mary's godson, and she had known them from their infancy. Similarly, she remembered her promise to her cousin, Frances, and released the Duke of Suffolk. Katherine Parr's brother, the Marquess of Northampton, was also set free in a relatively short time.

Charles V viewed this lenience with disapproval. She was being far too kind. She would never be able to keep order within her realm if people did not fear and respect her. As England's first queen regnant since the unfortunate Empress Matilda, she would be confronted with considerable masculine prejudice before she did anything at all. Even that redoubtable female ruler, the Queen Dowager, was later to tell the Emperor that 'a woman is never feared or respected as a man is, whatever her rank', and she went on, 'in time of war, in which these countries are more often engaged than is necessary, it is entirely impossible for a woman to govern satisfactorily. All she can do is to shoulder responsibility for mistakes committed by others . . . '

Both Mary and her councillors would have agreed with the Queen Dowager's statement that a woman's ability, 'compared with a man's, is as black compared with white', and the English statesmen told each other morosely that a female monarch would be disastrous for the country. They frightened her, these calculating, worldly men who were her councillors. Fiercely determined when her religion was threatened, she felt at a sad disadvantage in secular affairs, suspecting that she was an easy prey for the deceitful and the devious.

To make matters worse, the list of council members grew almost by the day, so many men were there to reward and placate. Some, like Sir Robert Rochester and Henry Jerningham, had always been her own loyal supporters. Others had served her father or her brother faithfully and had valuable experience, which she needed. Henry VIII's Keeper of the Privy Seal, John, Earl of Bedford, was still at his post and she kept him on, retaining also Edward VI's Lord Treasurer, the 1st Marquess of Winchester. The Earl of Arundel became her Lord Steward of the Household and she felt obliged to employ uncongenial people like Lord Rich, who had personally harried her about the Mass. There were far too many of them, and if they had argued and

*Mary, Queen Dowager of Hungary,* who ruled the Netherlands for her brother, Charles V, by an unknown artist, after Titian. (Rijksmuseum, Amsterdam)

*Stephen Gardiner, Bishop of Winchester,*
Mary's first Lord Chancellor, by an
unknown artist.
(The Master and Fellows of Trinity
College, Cambridge)

wrangled with each other before, they were even worse now. The Roman
Catholics hated the Protestants and there seemed to be innumerable old scores
to settle. If only Cardinal Pole had been in England, she could have relied upon
him, but he was far away, in Italy.

After considerable thought, she chose Stephen Gardiner, Bishop of Winchester, to be her Lord Chancellor, but she did not like him. The son of a
cloth-maker from Bury St Edmunds, he was a brilliant ecclesiastical lawyer, it
was true. He had been her father's principal secretary and he had undertaken
many important diplomatic missions abroad, riding tirelessly through France
and the Low Countries, attending interminable meetings and negotiating
complicated treaties.

He did, however, have his disadvantages. He was not the easiest colleague,
for he was intolerant and abrasive in manner: he and Lord Paget, his former
protégé, were at daggers drawn. Even more seriously, he had been in-
strumental in helping Henry VIII to divorce Mary's mother. He had even
written a book proving to his own satisfaction that Catherine of Aragon's
marriage was illegal. Mary could never forgive him for that.

His redeeming feature was that he was almost as anxious as she was herself
to restore the old religion. That was what she cared about most, that and the
vindication of her mother's memory. Even before leaving East Anglia, she had
written to Pope Julius III, asking him to lift the ecclesiastical censures against
England. She had told no one about this request, for she was convinced that if
her councillors knew what she was doing they would interfere and try to stop
her.

The situation was further complicated by Elizabeth. The past had destroyed
any hope that Mary would have a harmonious relationship with her half-
sister. In those first weeks she did her best. She led her along by the hand on
public occasions, put her in the place of honour and worried that the girl was
putting herself in danger of eternal damnation by being a heretic but, as the
days went by, Mary felt an increasing sense of unease. The precocious,
amusing child whom she had almost liked had grown into a haughty, wilful
young woman, distressingly reminiscent of Anne Boleyn. Elizabeth was tall

where Anne had been small and she was red-haired where her mother had been dark, but in manner there was a strong resemblance and Elizabeth seemed to have inherited 'the Concubine's' strange sense of humour, her delight in disconcerting and her self-absorbed ambition.

It was noticeable that although everyone else at court now obediently attended Mass with the Queen, Elizabeth and the Lutheran Anne of Cleves stayed away. Mary remonstrated with Anne, who immediately joined the services in the Chapel Royal, but Elizabeth remained obstinately absent for six weeks, until threats of the Tower forced her to seek an audience with the Queen.

They met in one of the galleries of Richmond Palace. When Elizabeth came in she knelt, as etiquette demanded, and she wept. She knew that she had lost the Queen's affection, she sobbed, but it was not her fault. On their father's orders she had been brought up in the Protestant faith and she knew no other. If she could have books and a learned man to instruct her, she would try to overcome her scruples about the Mass.

This was what Mary had hoped to hear, and she was delighted. For a short while all her reservations melted away. She could see that her sister was trembling with agitation. Surely she must be sincere. Promising her the books and the instructor she requested, she allowed Elizabeth to go back to her apartments and soon she was sending her gifts and treating her kindly again.

Elizabeth went to her first Mass on 9 September, the day after her twentieth birthday, but her manner was so resentful that Mary's suspicions came flooding back. Could it be true, as Simon Renard was continually warning her, that Elizabeth was plotting with the French, that she wanted Mary's throne for herself and that all the disaffected Protestants in the kingdom were looking to her for leadership? When Parliament met, the legislation to restore the old religion might founder if Elizabeth were allowed to make trouble.

Renard was, indeed, remarkably pessimistic about Mary's prospects, and he told his friend, the Bishop of Arras, one of Charles V's principal advisers, 'I know the Queen to be good, easily influenced, inexpert in worldly matters and a novice all round, and the English so grasping that if one cares to try them with presents and promises one may do what one likes with them . . . I believe that if God does not preserve her, she will be deceived and lost, either by the machinations of the French, the conspiracies of the English, by poison or otherwise.' There was only one way out of her difficulties. The Queen would have to marry.

# 6

## MARY THE QUEEN

*F*ROM THE VERY MOMENT that the Emperor had heard of Mary's miraculous accession, he had been pondering the question of her marriage, and indeed he had told his ambassadors that as well as congratulating her they must 'point out to her that it will be necessary, in order to be supported in the labour of governing and assisted in matters that are not of ladies' capacity, that she soon contracts matrimony with the person who shall appear to her the most fit from the above point of view'. He would, of course, be happy to advise her 'with all affectionate sincerity'.

Brought up by his extremely effective aunt, Margaret of Austria, and accustomed to his equally efficient sister, the Queen Dowager, and his highly intelligent daughters, the Emperor knew perfectly well that governing a country was not beyond a woman's capabilities. He knew Mary's weaknesses, however, and he believed that for her own sake she needed the support of a husband. Naturally, his main preoccupation was that she should marry the right person. An unmarried female monarch would immediately be wooed by all manner of ambitious men, and it was vital that she should choose someone who had the Empire's interests at heart.

The matter became particularly pressing when he heard that there was already an important English contender for her hand. Edward Courtenay, son of Mary's old friend the Marchioness of Exeter, seemed to many of his fellow countrymen to be the ideal consort for the Queen. She had been delighted to see him that day when she released the prisoners from the Tower, for the poor lad had spent most of his life there.

He had only been eight when his father had been executed for treason

Charles V's portable altar.
(The Escorial, Madrid: photograph authorised by the Patrimonio Nacional)

together with Cardinal Pole's father, and he and his mother had been shut up in that grim fortress. The Marchioness was allowed to employ tutors for him, and he was carefully educated in the classics. He showed a gift for music and the arts, and his fellow prisoner, the Bishop of Winchester, had latterly been taking a kindly interest in him.

Now a tall, handsome young man of twenty-three, Edward instantly became an object of romantic speculation. Although Mary did not realise it at first, everyone believed that she would marry him, in spite of the difference in their ages for, as a descendant of the House of York, he seemed a most suitable husband. When, out of kindness, she granted him a handsome London residence, people told each other that this was a sure sign of her intentions. When she sent one of her gentlemen to guide him through the unfamiliar maze of court life, they were even more certain than ever that he was being groomed for his future role as King. His mother, they knew, as one of Mary's favourite ladies-in-waiting, often shared the royal bed at night. No doubt the two women lay and had long, nocturnal discussions about an impending wedding.

Many people favoured the lad because they had a horror of the Queen taking a foreign husband. They could not abide the thought of being ruled by a stranger. It was bad enough when a King took a foreign wife. There were foreign courtiers, foreign attendants, foreign visitors with their strange ways and their expensive requirements. How much worse it would be, were Mary to find a husband abroad. Before they knew it, he would be appointing his own people to the offices of state, trying to enforce strange, outlandish laws and abolishing Englishmen's ancient liberties.

Mary soon realised what was being said, for her Lord Chancellor was continually singing Courtenay's praises, but when the Bishop openly urged her to look favourably upon his protégé, she gave him an evasive answer. The boy was still very young, she said, and had yet to show his true nature.

Indeed, she had recently received disquieting reports that he was enjoying the pleasures of his new-found freedom with all too much enthusiasm. Casting aside the courtier she had so helpfully sent to him, he had started visiting prostitutes.

Nothing, in fact, was further from Mary's mind than marrying Courtenay. As far as she was concerned, he was too lowly in rank, for he was her subject. Apart from that, he was too young, and in any event she expected to find her husband elsewhere. Simon Renard had raised the question of her marriage that first evening at Beaulieu. She had shown little apparent interest, but she had spoken as though she expected the Emperor to choose her consort for her. She only begged him to remember that she was now thirty-seven years old, adding that she would not wish to marry someone she had never met. Charles V was not yet ready to disclose his thoughts, but he had already made his choice, and on 30 July 1553 he had dispatched a letter to his son Philip, suggesting that he should marry the Queen of England.

Prince Philip had been born in Spain when Mary was eleven, and he lived there still. The Emperor had spent the first years of own married life in that country with his Portuguese wife, who was also his cousin. A year after their wedding, the Empress Isabella had given birth to their son, and from that moment Charles took a close and devoted interest in his heir. He did not see very much of him, of course, for the exigencies of warfare and the need to rule his vast inheritance had taken him away to Italy and the Low Countries. However, he received regular reports of the Prince's progress.

When Philip was seven he was taught to read and write. Later, fifty aristocratic pages were selected to share his education, tutors were appointed, and he began to study Latin, Greek, architecture, mathematics, geography and history. For some reason he received no instruction in modern languages. French was Charles V's principal tongue, but he must have judged it more important for his heir to speak Latin, the language of diplomacy and the Church.

Philip disliked mathematics but he loved reading, music and drawing and at thirteen he was choosing books for himself, as well as ordering a volume of large sheets of plain paper 'which his Highness asked for so that he could paint in it'. He was also allowed to play cards and quoits, and from an early age he was taught to shoot wolves, bear, deer and rabbits with his crossbow. He did so with such deadly accuracy that his father made a rule forbidding him to kill more than a stated number of animals each week.

Philip was twelve when his mother died in childbirth and, in the absence of his father, he was chief mourner at her funeral. The Emperor now began to send him frequent letters and instructions. The Prince must trust no one, Charles impressed upon him, for even the most outwardly helpful courtier might have ulterior motives. He should guard himself carefully, never show any weakness or betray any emotion lest someone take advantage of him. His routine should be fixed and his days carefully planned. He must be just, devout and God-fearing. Another boy might have rebelled, but Philip, shy and sensitive, read his father's orders gravely and grew up to be serious, decorous and reserved. 'Up till now,' Charles told him in 1543, 'thanks be to God, there is nothing obvious to criticise in you', but he continued his careful supervision.

By the age of sixteen, Philip was ruling Spain as its Regent and he had married his cousin, the Infanta Maria of Portugal, amidst a flurry of fresh

*The Empress Isabella*, mother of Philip II of Spain, a posthumous portrait by Titian.
(All rights reserved © the Prado, Madrid)

admonitions from his anxious parent. He must remember that he was not marrying to enjoy sex but to produce heirs. He should not lie too often with his wife, for frequent intercourse could stunt his growth. Needless to say, he was not to seek the company of other women either.

Philip did as he was told. In spite of his restraint, his wife was pregnant by the end of 1544 and, on Thursday 9 July, he was able to send a joyful message to his father announcing the birth of a son, whom they would name Charles, after him. (The child was to be better known to history as Don Carlos.) Both mother and child were doing well, but the following day the Princess was feverish and by Sunday she was critically ill. The Prince was at her bedside, the doctors bled her and gave her stimulants, but from delirium she lapsed into unconsciousness and she died that afternoon. Deeply upset, Philip withdrew to a monastery and saw no one for several weeks.

Fortunately, the baby continued to make good progress and in the years that followed, Philip did not show any sign of wishing to marry again. He did, however, form a liaison with a lady named Doña Isabel de Osario, and was so faithful to her that people thought he had secretly made her his wife. His father was almost certainly aware of the relationship, but he turned a blind eye to it. Given time, Philip would undoubtedly remarry, but in the meantime his education in statesmanship had to continue and his future must be secured.

The title of Holy Roman Emperor was not hereditary. Emperors were elected by the German princes and, if Philip wished to succeed to that honour, he must cultivate them. When he was twenty-one, Charles therefore told him to come to Brussels. There he would make useful contacts, and father and son could have long discussions about the problems of government. He should come by way of Italy in order to see something of the world.

*Don Carlos*, son of Philip, by A S Coello, 1564.
(Kunsthistorisches Museum, Vienna)

*Charles V and Prince Philip bearing up the world*, a wood engraving of a triumphal arch erected for Philip's entry into Antwerp in 1549.
(By permission of the British Library)

Obedient as ever, the Prince set off with his retinue and the fine musicians who went with him everywhere. He travelled first to Genoa and then to Milan, where he met the famous artist, Titian, and sat for his portrait. After that, he turned north by way of Innsbruck, Munich and Heidelberg for Brussels. He arrived there on 1 April 1549, to be reunited with his father for the first time in six years.

Philip was enjoying his journey immensely. His early love of drawing had become a passion for collecting paintings, he was greatly taken with the red-brick houses and the beautiful formal gardens of the Low Countries, and he enlisted the services of various musicians whom he encountered at the courts of his father and his aunt. Unfortunately, his future subjects were not impressed with him. His inability to speak any language but Spanish was a great disadvantage, as was his natural reserve. 'They take his taciturnity and retiring manners for ignorance,' the Bishop of Arras told the Queen Dowager, and she replied that she hoped to hear that her nephew was attempting to be more affable and was making some effort to learn French.

No doubt these reproofs were conveyed to Philip, for he did his best with the Electors, speaking to them in fluent Latin, going out hunting with them and even trying to improve his image by drinking the local ale. Unfortunately, many of the German princes were Lutheran and they remained determinedly unimpressed. Moreover, a family crisis forced Charles to abandon his dream of Philip becoming Emperor. His own brother, Ferdinand, King of the Romans, was determined to secure that position for himself and he even wanted to pass it on to his son, Maximilian. The family quarrel was only made up when it was agreed that Ferdinand could put himself forward as a candidate for the Empire when Charles died, on the understanding that Philip would be the next choice after him instead of Maximilian.

With no visible regrets, the Prince returned to Spain and settled down happily to rule the country with meticulous attention to detail, treated by his father as an equal, now, not a pupil. He resumed his relationship with Doña Isabel, laid out formal gardens like those he had seen in Brussels, assembled an extensive library, corresponded with Titian, patronised other leading masters of the day, listened to music and attended Mass. He was grave, courteous and kind-hearted, and if his life lacked spontaneity, then he preferred it that way.

His father continued to worry about his future, however, and in the spring of 1553 he decided that Philip ought to take another wife. 'It is now a long time since the death of the Princess (whom God receive in His glory)', he wrote, 'and it seems to me suitable and necessary that you should marry again, because of your age and because of the progeny which I hope God may grant you.' Don Carlos was a healthy boy of nearly eight, but one prince was not enough. Charles was tired, his health was poor and he longed to abdicate and retire to a monastery to end his days in peace, but he must first make sure that the succession was secure.

At that point, Philip was almost betrothed to his cousin, the Infanta Maria. Her father was King Manuel of Portugal and her mother was Charles's sister Eleanor. In the Habsburg web of intermarriage, she was also the aunt of Philip's first wife. Preliminary discussions were begun, but three months later came England's miracle, and an unmarried Queen regnant was suddenly in need of a husband. It seemed almost too good to be true. If Philip could marry Mary, the French would be unable to meddle in England, the sea route

*Eleanor of Austria*, Charles V's sister, by Van Cleve.
(The Duke of Buccleuch and Queensberry KT, Drumlanrig Castle, Dumfriesshire)

*The Infanta Maria of Portugal*, Eleanor of Austria's daughter, whom Philip considered marrying, by François Clouet.
(Photographie Giraudon, Musée Condé, Chantilly)

between Spain and the Netherlands would be secure and Philip's own position would be enhanced. He might never be Holy Roman Emperor, but he could be the King of England who brought that country back into the Roman Catholic Church.

Charles therefore wrote his letter to Spain. He himself was the most obvious husband for Mary, he said, for they had been betrothed long years before and he felt sure that the English 'would more readily support me than any other, for they have always shown a liking for me'. However, his health and age were such that he could not contemplate matrimony again 'and it has occurred to me that if they were to make a proposal to me, we might delay in such a manner as to suggest to their minds the possibility of approaching you.' Philip was perhaps too far advanced in his negotiations for the Infanta Maria, of course, and his father was merely mentioning the possibility, but it was worth considering.

Philip recognised an order when he saw it, and he moved with uncharacteristic speed. Within days of receiving his father's letter, he was composing his reply. The Emperor's message had arrived at exactly the right moment, he said, for he had just decided to break off the Portuguese business as the dowry was too low. 'All I have left to say about the English affair is that I am rejoiced to hear that my aunt has come to the throne in that kingdom.' (Mary was actually Philip's first cousin once removed, of course, but she was of his father's generation and he always referred to her by that inaccurate title.) In short, 'if you wish to arrange the match for me, you know that I am so obedient a son that I have no will other than yours, especially in a matter of such high import. Therefore I think best to leave all to Your Majesty to dispose as shall seem most fitting.' The plan could go ahead.

There were difficulties in the way, of course. The Portuguese would be annoyed, Charles's sister would be furious because her daughter had been slighted, the King of the Romans would be equally angry because he wanted his son to marry Mary, Henry II of France would do all he could to foil the scheme, Mary might be reluctant and the English would certainly be hostile to the notion of a foreign consort, but the benefits were so plain to see that everything possible must be done to ensure that the plan succeeded.

While Simon Renard waited for definite instructions, the whole English court was buzzing with rumours about Mary marrying Edward Courtenay, the King of the Romans, the Prince of Piedmont, even Cardinal Pole. When Renard asked her about Courtenay, the Queen was quick to reassure him. She had only spoken to him once, the day she had pardoned him. The ambassador mentioned various other possibilities, but she was equally uninterested. They were all too young, she said, and she was 'old enough to be their mother'. It was a pity, she added casually, that Prince Philip was betrothed to the Princess of Portugal, and she went on to tell Renard that she had never 'felt that which was called love, nor harboured thoughts of voluptuousness', and had never considered marriage until God had pleased to raise her to the throne, but she would obey Charles V's wishes in the matter as if he were her father.

This was most encouraging, although that same night Monsieur de Noailles, the French ambassador, got wind of the Emperor's scheme and sent instant word to his own master. Henry II was furious. A marriage between Mary and an imperial candidate would be a 'perpetual calamity' for the whole of Christendom, he said, and he gave immediate orders that everything possible was to be done to break the match. Monsieur de Noailles should support Edward Courtenay, the Lady Elizabeth, or indeed anyone else likely to make trouble for the Emperor.

By 20 September, Charles had Philip's agreement to their plan, and he instructed Renard accordingly. Mary, however, had other matters on her mind, for she was deeply involved in the preparations for her coronation. Any further discussion of her marriage plans would have to wait until after the ceremony.

On 27 September 1553, she took up residence in the Tower. The following day, she summoned her Privy Councillors to a special meeting. Usually, they knelt to her but, to their astonishment, she sank to her knees before them and

*Antoine de Noailles*, the French ambassador, engraved by P L van Schuppen. (Bibliothèque Nationale, Paris)

Psalter covered in crimson velvet, presented to Mary in 1553.
(By courtesy of the Trustees of the British Museum)

began a lengthy and impassioned speech about her miraculous accession to the throne, the duties of Kings and Queens, and her solemn intention of carrying out her God-given task to His greater glory, the public good and the benefit of all her subjects. The councillors were so moved that they wept. 'No one knew how to answer, amazed as they all were by this humble and lowly discourse, so unlike anything ever heard before in England, and by the Queen's great goodness and integrity,' reported Renard who, as usual, heard an account of the occasion from Mary herself.

Overwhelmed by the magnitude of her responsibilities, she was in a state of nervous apprehension and she had been worrying for days about the coronation and all the attendant ceremonies. Who would officiate? She had just consigned Archbishop Cranmer to the Tower for publicly opposing the restoration of the Mass, and the Archbishop of York was completely out of favour. Her Chancellor would have to perform the ceremony, in his capacity as Bishop of Winchester, but would she be able to take the coronation oath? What would she do if it contained some reference to the new religion, as well it might, since England was still officially a Protestant kingdom?

It may have been the Bishop who sensibly suggested that she should study the text of the oath in advance. She duly sent for it and scrutinised the wording. It seemed acceptable, but she would be promising to observe the laws of England. Those laws included Edward VI's Protestant legislation and she could never swear to that. One of her advisers suggested that she could amend the wording. She could say 'the just and licit laws of England', which would imply that she was not swearing to obey those which she regarded as unjust and illegal. After further heart-searching, she settled for that.

There still remained the problem of the holy oil for the anointing. Any oil currently in England was bound to be contaminated, because it would have been consecrated while the country lay under the Pope's censures. Simon Renard found the solution to that difficulty. He wrote urgently to Brussels, and

*Antoine Perrenot Granvelle, Bishop of Arras*, Charles V's Secretary of State, by Antonis Mor, 1549.
(Kunsthistorisches Museum, Vienna)

the Bishop of Arras obligingly sent over three phials containing the sacred oil he himself used, with apologies for their plain containers. He had not had time to commission anything more regal, he explained.

The Queen Dowager was also eager to be of service, and when she heard that Mary liked nothing better than a piece of wild boar, she arranged to have a fine specimen killed and sent over for the coronation feast. The French ambassador reported that Charles V himself had shot the boar with his own harquebus, but that was merely one of his jealous imaginings. Charles V with his many ailments was in no condition to go out hunting, nor would Mary have expected it. She always addressed the Emperor with almost exaggerated deference, and a gift from his sister gave her pleasure enough.

The Queen Dowager's gesture was particularly cheering when everything else was proving so difficult. No sooner was one problem solved than another three sprang up. Some of Mary's Privy Councillors came to her and said that Parliament should meet before her coronation, not afterwards. Bewildered, she asked them why, and was told that this would be the safest course to adopt in case she was assassinated as she travelled through the streets of London to Westminster Abbey. Unfortunate though that would be, at least her legislation would have gone through.

Not unnaturally, Mary was distressed. She knew perfectly well this was a ploy to strengthen Parliament's authority at the expense of her own. If Parliament met before she was crowned, it would look as though she owed her position to them instead of the reverse. She rejected the suggestion, but she was left in a state of alarm about her own personal safety and her other Privy Councillors had great difficulty in reassuring her. There would be searches for arms, they said, and she would have a strong guard with her. No fanatical Protestant would be able to come near her. Even so it was disquieting, all the more so because there had already been a plot to murder the Bishop of Winchester and he had come to lodge in her palace for safety.

In the event, everything went smoothly when she left the Tower on

86

30 September for her formal entry into London. She was wearing a blue velvet gown trimmed with ermine. On her head was a gold, trellis-work cap set with jewels and pearls, and an ornate gem-studded gold garland. With her red-gold hair and her pink and white complexion she was pretty still, even if she did look tired and the cap and garland were so heavy that she had to prop her head up with her hands. She took her place in a chariot covered in cloth of gold, beneath a canopy of state. The six horses pulling her chariot moved off and they were on their way.

The streets had been strewn with flowers, and people had hung tapestries from their windows as they always did on such occasions. In front of the Queen rode a lengthy cavalcade of knights, gentlemen and judges, doctors of divinity and bishops, Privy Councillors and peers. The Lord Chancellor was with the Lord High Treasurer, the Earl of Oxford bore the sword of state and Sir Edward Hastings led the Queen's own riderless horse in its rich trappings.

Somewhere in the procession was Edward Courtenay, looking distinctly surly. At vast expense he had ordered a special blue suit for that day, trimmed with goldwork. Somehow or other the Queen had got to hear about it and she had sent him a curt message forbidding him to wear it. Blue was her own special colour and if people saw him arrayed in it, they would immediately conclude that he was her accepted suitor. Behind Mary's chariot came two other carriages. In the first, lined with cloth of silver, sat Elizabeth and Anne of Cleves, facing each other. In the next were other female royal relatives, and beside them rode forty-six ladies-in-waiting clad in crimson satin.

Through cheering crowds, the cavalcade made its way along the streets of London, pausing every now and again so that the Queen could admire an elaborate pageant or hear a welcoming speech. At Fenchurch Street, the Genoese merchants lifted a child up in a chair to make a loyal address. At Gracechurch corner, wine flowed from an artificial mountain and four children on its summit welcomed the Queen. A little further on, the Florentine merchants had excelled themselves. At the top of their high scaffolding, an angel clad in green raised a trumpet to his lips and appeared to play. The fanfare actually emanated from a musician cunningly concealed below. Large cloth-of-silver placards bore complimentary verses in Latin, with an English translation for the benefit of the multitude, and six persons in long, coloured gowns and high-crowned hats made flattering speeches to Mary.

Double-barrelled wheel-lock pistol of Charles V, made in Munich about 1540–5.
(All rights reserved, the Metropolitan Museum of Art, New York, gift of William H Riggs, 1913: 14.25.1425)

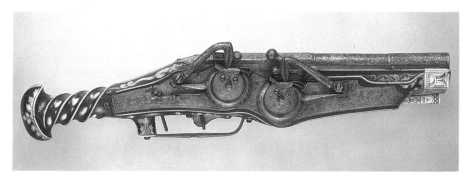

As her chariot reached Cornhill, trumpets sounded, more children made speeches and she was presented with a purse containing a thousand pounds, 'which she most thankfully received'. The children drawn up outside St Paul's schoolhouse had verses to sing to her, but attention was distracted from them by the daring feat being performed far above their heads. At the very top of the spire of St Paul's a Dutchman named Peter was perched on the weather-cock. While Mary and everyone else held their breath, he first of all waved a little flag, then he stood on one leg and shook the other. As a *pièce de résistance*, he knelt down on the weathercock's back, 'to the great marvel and wondering of all the people which beheld him', said a chronicler, who wrote an account of the proceedings that day. After this, even the spectacle of little children with tapers wafting sweet perfumes towards Her Majesty from outside the Dean's house seemed rather an anticlimax, but the procession continued to wind its way onwards and amidst all the cheering there was no hint of Protestant dissent.

Next morning, Mary went to Westminster Abbey for her coronation. She walked the short distance from Westminster Palace, treading on a blue carpet specially laid for the occasion, between railings erected to keep back the crowds. She was accompanied by those bishops loyal to her, and she wore a great crimson velvet mantle with a long train borne by her Chamberlain and by the Duchess of Norfolk.

When she reached the abbey, the Bishop of Winchester and the other officiating clergy received her, beneath a golden canopy. Bells pealed, trumpets sounded, the great organ played and the choristers sang. All the peers and peeresses were in their ermine-trimmed robes and the gentlemen of the royal household were decked out in either scarlet satin or crimson velvet, according to rank. In the place of honour, before them all, stood Lady Elizabeth, her scarlet mantle over an ermine-trimmed gown with an extra-long train, a small gold crown on her red hair. She pointedly ignored the imperial ambassadors,

*Old St Paul's*, engraved by W Hollar in 1657.
(By courtesy of the Trustees of the British Museum)

Clock salt belonging to Henry VIII and in the
royal collection during Mary's reign.
(The Worshipful Company of Goldsmiths,
London)

Michaelmas Plea Roll, 1553, showing Mary
enthroned, before scenes of
Northumberland's revolt.
(Public Record Office, KB27/1168)

but she had a charming smile and gracious words for their French colleague every time she passed him.

The entire floor of the abbey had been covered with blue cloth, and a high platform had been erected before the altar. The Bishop of Winchester led Mary to each of its four corners, saying to the congregation, 'If any man will or can allege any cause why Queen Mary should not be crowned, let them speak now!' For a moment there was silence, and then the assembled company acclaimed her with one voice, shouting triumphantly, 'Queen Mary! Queen Mary!'

Having changed her garments for a robe of white taffeta beneath a mantle of purple velvet, Mary sat down upon the coronation chair. The Bishop of Winchester anointed her with the special oil brought from Brussels and then he placed three crowns upon her head, one after the other, as Tudor coronation ritual required. The first was St Edward's crown, the second was the imperial gold crown of England and the third was a very rich crown made specially for her. It weighed more than seven pounds, and inside it was a purple cap of state. The *Te Deum* was sung, Elizabeth and all the peers swore an oath of loyalty to her, and then Mary knelt while the Bishop sang Mass. Her own crown was upon her head and in each hand she held a sceptre: the king's and the one usually given to a queen consort.

It was almost five o'clock in the afternoon before the ceremony was over and, exhausted, she walked from the abbey in her purple mantle, the crown still upon her head, the king's sceptre in one hand and in the other the orb, 'which she twirled and turned in her hand as she came homeward'. The Great Hall of Westminster Palace, so recently the scene of the Duke of Northumberland's trial, had been set with long tables for the coronation banquet, and she took her place beneath her canopy of state. At the same table, but a respectful distance away, sat Elizabeth and Anne of Cleves on one side, and the Bishop of Winchester on the other.

The Duke of Norfolk, as Earl Marshal, and the Earl of Arundel, as Lord Steward, supervised the proceedings on horseback, and no fewer than three hundred and twelve dishes were set before the Queen by the dignitaries who served her. Her champion rode into the hall to throw down his gauntlet in the traditional challenge to any who might oppose her, and she drank his health from a gold cup, which she then presented to him.

Outside, the hundreds of people who had watched the comings and goings scrambled on the ground to tear up the blue carpet and snatch at the vast quantities of waste food thrown out from the kitchens. They even tore down the railings and carried them away too. It was late in the evening when Mary finally thanked the foreign ambassadors for attending, and retired to her own apartments, while her excited subjects still sang and cheered outside.

# 7

## PHILIP

*T*HE CORONATION ceremony had been a deeply emotional occasion for Mary, and just four days later Parliament met to enact, she hoped, the legislation she was so anxious to introduce. The first session did little in the way of actual business. There was a new Treason Bill, followed by two other bills restoring the Courtenay family to their honours and estates. Needless to say, these were instantly interpreted by the public as a prelude to the Queen's marriage, but in fact they were merely the result of her friendship with the Marchioness of Exeter and her anxiety to make everything as it had been, before Anne Boleyn and the infamous divorce.

The second session opened three days later, and the real business began. An act was passed without difficulty declaring Catherine of Aragon's marriage to Henry VIII to have been perfectly legal, but the other principal measure met with much resistance. All Edward VI's religious legislation was to be repealed, including the act permitting the marriage of priests and, of course, his Act of Uniformity. There was a fierce debate in the House of Commons, lasting for

*La Gloria*, the altarpiece commissioned by Charles V in 1551, which shows Charles, his wife and Philip towards the top right.

91

eight hours, and although the Queen's supporters had a large majority when the vote came, the intensity of the resistance was a sign that Protestant dissent was not going to vanish quietly.

Mary did not seem to take much note of that. She had been persuaded to postpone introducing the legislation restoring England's links with Rome, but at least a good beginning had been made and the Pope had delighted her by making Cardinal Pole his legate to England. Soon her old friend would be able to come home after his long exile and he would help her to achieve her cherished ambitions. By then, she also expected to have an even more important ally by her side: her husband. As soon as the coronation celebrations were over she would see Simon Renard and learn whom the Emperor had chosen for her. She shrank from the notion of sexual intercourse with a stranger, she was probably frightened at the idea of childbirth at her advanced age, but she knew what she had to do. God had made her Queen of England, and she was certain that He would in time perform another miracle and send her a son to succeed her.

The Emperor had agreed that when his extraordinary ambassadors returned home, Simon Renard should stay on in England, replacing Jean Scheyfve as resident ambassador. Renard was admitted to the Queen's presence on 7 October, to present his letters of credence. This was an entirely formal occasion, but a few days later he was invited to a private audience and, after the usual polite preliminaries, he came swiftly to the point. The Emperor would gladly have married Mary himself, he said, had not years and infirmity rendered him 'a poor thing to be offered to her'. Charles had therefore decided that he could provide no better substitute than his son and heir, Prince Philip.

The words said at last, Renard waited expectantly for a torrent of gratitude. After all, Mary had already seemed to be hinting that Philip would be a welcome bridegroom, and she would surely be both honoured and delighted now that the proposal had been made. For a long moment she gazed at him in silence, and then she said stiffly that she thanked the Emperor for suggesting a 'greater match than she deserved'. However, she went on, she did not know how her subjects would take to a foreign consort, the Privy Council might not

Philip's breviary.
(The Escorial, Madrid: photograph authorised by the Patrimonio Nacional)

consent, Philip would probably spend all his time abroad, England could be dragged into foreign wars and, worse still, she had heard that the Prince was 'not as wise' as the Emperor 'and was very young, being only twenty-six years of age'. If he were disposed to be amorous, such was not her desire. She could not possibly make up her mind at once, she concluded, but in case he thought she was committed elsewhere, she hastened to reassure him that she was as free as the day of her birth and had 'never taken a fancy to anyone'.

Astounded at this lack of enthusiasm, Renard sprang instantly to Philip's defence. As he told Charles V afterwards, he had immediately pointed out that the Prince was 'so admirable, so virtuous, prudent and modest as to appear too wonderful to be human' and, although Mary might think he was exaggerating, 'I was in reality minimising his qualities.' Far from being young and ardent, 'His Highness was middle-aged, being twenty-six … had already been married, had a son of eight and was a prince of so stable and settled a character that he was no longer young, for nowadays a man nearly thirty was considered as old as men formerly were at forty.'

Even this valiant eulogy failed to convince her, and a day or two later she summoned him again. Could she please have a written summary of the main points he had made about the marriage, she asked, and then, taking him impetuously by the hand, she begged him to tell her if all he had said about Philip was really true, whether he was indeed 'of even temper, of balanced judgment and well-conditioned.' Renard assured her that he was. The Prince had 'qualities as virtuous as any Prince in this world'. Mary pressed his hand, murmuring, 'That is well,' but her fears were not allayed. Perhaps Renard was speaking out of affection for Philip, or even from fear of him? Would it not be possible for her to see the Prince for herself before she made up her mind?

It would not, said Renard, knowing full well that the Emperor would never risk sending his son to face a possible rebuff in front of the whole world. He was sure, he added smoothly, that the Prince would come to England to marry her as soon as he heard that she had accepted him. But what of the weather, cried Mary, at this bad time of year, what of the dangerous seas, and what of the French, who would surely try to stop him?

There was really no answering her nervous fears, and of course her apprehension was made all the worse by Courtenay's supporters who were trying to blacken the Prince's character. Even his own subjects disliked Philip, they said, for his 'excessive pride and small wisdom', and Renard had to make a long speech countering that, too. It was all very frustrating, and Renard was glad when Charles V's formal, written proposal for his son arrived and he was able to take it to the Queen on 28 October. Surely that would reassure her once and for all.

He wisely took the precaution of showing her the letter in advance, so that its contents would not take her by surprise when she read the document in the presence of her councillors. He now handed it to her solemnly, hoping for an encouraging reply, but she was in a highly emotional state and she could hardly trust herself to speak. She did manage to murmur a few private words as he handed her the packet, for the Privy Councillors who were with her were standing at a respectful distance away and were out of earshot.

She had wept for over two hours that very day, she whispered, as she prayed to God to help her to make up her mind, and she believed now that she would agree to the Emperor's suggestion. A wave of relief swept over Renard. There was a long way to go yet, but his mission would be successfully

Mary's copy of Plutarch's *Bioi paralleloi*, printed in Basle in 1553.
(The Royal Collection © 1993 Her Majesty The Queen)

accomplished. He made a few suitable remarks to the councillors, Mary gazed at him earnestly and breathed 'Believe!' then she retired to her chamber.

The following day was a Sunday, but in the evening she sent for him. He found her alone, except for Mrs Clarentius, and he saw that the Holy Sacrament was displayed on an altar in the room. Mary said that she had not slept since he had first shown her the Emperor's letter, but had continually wept and prayed to God for guidance, invoking the Holy Sacrament as her protector, guide and counsellor. With that, she knelt before the altar, and Renard and Mrs Clarentius hastily sank to their knees too. There was a long silence, and then the Queen suddenly exclaimed, *'Veni creator spiritus!'* Rising to her feet, she turned to tell them that she felt she had been inspired by God to promise to marry the Prince, and she would do so now, solemnly, before the Holy Sacrament. Her mind was made up, she said, and she would never change it. She would love Philip perfectly and she would never give him any cause to feel jealous.

Renard went away triumphant, only to receive one of her little notes saying, 'I forgot to ask you one question the other night; that is to say, are you quite sure that there has never been any contract concerning marriage between the Prince and the daughter of Portugal, for there was much talk to that effect', and if that was all right, then how was she to break the news to her Privy Council? There was no agreement with the Portuguese Princess, the ambassador replied soothingly, and as to the councillors, she should wait until they asked her what was happening rather than raising the subject herself.

All the recent agitation had left Mary feeling 'heavy' and ill. Renard was told that the weather was to blame. The French ambassador heard a different story. The Queen suffered this way every year, his spies told him, with palpitations so constant that she could do nothing but weep. 'They say it comes from the womb,' he added significantly, though whether this was a spiteful allusion to the unlikeliness that she would bear children, or whether it was the true cause is impossible to say. Perhaps this particular bout of ill health had a physical basis, but it may have been the result of stress. Whatever the reason, she kept to her chamber for a week, during which time Renard made it his business to have long talks with all the leading councillors, holding out promises and giving dire warnings about what would happen were the French allowed a foothold in England.

By 8 November he had done his work, Mary was feeling better, and the leading Privy Councillors were summoned to hear her give her formal reply to the Emperor's letter. The Bishop of Winchester, Lord Arundel, the Bishop of Norwich, Lord Paget and Sir William Petre were all present. Following a carefully prearranged plan, Renard read out Charles V's letter offering Philip, and the Queen, 'with a royal mien, becoming modesty, a timid countenance and trembling gesture' led them into another apartment to confer with them, 'dissembling as if she had never heard the question mentioned before'. No doubt they kept up a similar pretence.

Finally, they all came back. Smiling at last, she said that she was grateful to His Majesty, and she would accept the Prince. Renard noted with satisfaction, 'It seems that she is beginning to understand what love is, for she is always overjoyed to hear His Highness spoken of', and indeed Mary herself accused Renard teasingly of making her fall in love with Philip, adding wistfully that the Prince might not be obliged to him for that, though she would do her best to please him in every way.

Always afraid that she might change her mind, Renard now had the happy inspiration of sending for a picture of Philip so that she could see what he looked like, even if she could not yet meet him. The Queen Dowager, a notable art collector, was prevailed upon to send over a portrait painted by Titian in the spring of 1551. 'Unfortunately the picture has suffered to some extent from the passage of time and also from its transport here from Augsburg,' she explained. 'Nevertheless, the Queen [Mary] will obtain a sufficient idea of what he looks like by studying the portrait in the correct light and at some little distance, for the said Titian's works are all of that kind. On a close view, the sitter cannot be recognised.'

She allowed the picture to go to London on condition that it be returned to her again, 'as it is only a dead thing, when she has the living model in her presence', and Mary gladly agreed. Art historians have argued about which picture it is, but it seems possible it may be the portrait eventually bequeathed by the Queen Dowager to Philip himself and now hanging in the Prado in Madrid.

Far from losing interest in the match, Mary seemed to be gaining confidence at the very thought of her impending marriage. It was still being kept secret from the public, but she was showing a new firmness in her dealings with her advisers. Rather than being intimidated when the Speaker of the House of Commons led a deputation of noblemen and members of his own house to urge her to marry an Englishman, she was so irritated by his long, rambling discourse that instead of letting the Chancellor reply for her, as she should have done, she burst into speech herself, exclaiming that Parliament was not accustomed to use such language to the Kings of England, and that monarchs could marry whom they chose.

Those present were surprised and amused by her sudden boldness, and Lord Arundel laughingly told the Bishop of Winchester that he had lost his post of Chancellor since the Queen had usurped it. Mary remained angry, however, and the next time she saw the Bishop she accused him of having inspired the Speaker's oration. She would never marry Edward Courtenay, she said bluntly. With tears in his eyes, the Bishop explained that he had been fond of the lad, since they were in prison together. Would it be suitable, snapped Mary, to force her to marry a man simply because the Bishop had conceived a friendship for him in prison? He hung his head and admitted that

*Sir William Petre*, Secretary of
State, by Van der Meulen, 1567.
(National Portrait Gallery,
London)

Philip's copy of *Acerca De
Materia Medicinal*, 1555, by
Pedacio Dioscorides.
(Biblioteca Nacional, Madrid)

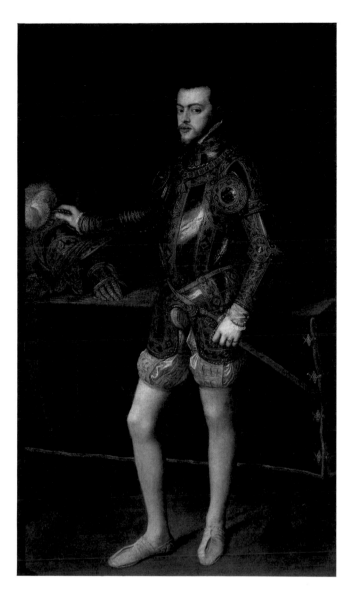

it would not, and from that day onwards he reconciled himself to the notion of the Spanish marriage.

Even fresh rumours of Philip's alleged voluptuousness and numerous, fictitious, bastard children could not deflect Mary now. The religious legislation and the bill for invalidating her mother's divorce were going through Parliament and her thoughts were much on the past. When asked to choose a name for the baby daughter of one of her nobles, she at once selected Catherine, pointing out that it had been her own mother's name. The recollection of all that had gone before was strengthening her determination that her half-sister Elizabeth should never succeed her. Lady Margaret Douglas, now Lady Lennox, had recently arrived back at court after giving birth to her latest child, and Mary began to give her precedence over Elizabeth, telling Renard and Lord Paget that her sister could never have her throne because of her heretical opinions, illegitimacy and characteristics in which she resembled her mother.

*Henry II of France*, by Clouet.
(Bibliothèque Nationale, Paris)

Fearing that if Elizabeth were removed from the succession, Henry II of France would put forward his son's fiancée, Mary, Queen of Scots, Renard begged Mary to hide her antipathy towards her half-sister, but it was no easy task. 'I had much trouble in persuading the Queen to dissemble,' he reported, 'for she still resents the injuries inflicted on Queen Catherine, her lady mother, by the machinations of Anne Boleyn, mother of Elizabeth, and recalls trouble and unpleasantness before and since her accession, unrest and disagreeable occurrences, to which Elizabeth has given rise.'

He persuaded her at last, however, and at the beginning of December, shortly after Mary dissolved Parliament, she gave Elizabeth permission to leave court. Paget and Arundel were sent to warn the girl of the consequences should she plot with the French, but when she and Mary took leave of each other they did so with false smiles and expressions of good will, the Queen

Henry II's shield.
(All rights reserved, the Metropolitan Museum of Art, New York, Harris Brisbane Dick Fund, 1934: 34.85)

presenting Elizabeth with a beautiful sable cap. Soon, very soon, Prince Philip would be coming, Mary believed, they would marry, and if God sent them their son, she would no longer have to fear the duplicity of Anne Boleyn's child.

On 2 January 1554 the Emperor's special ambassadors, led by Count Egmont, arrived in London with the draft marriage articles. In the previous few weeks, Mary, Renard and Lord Paget had worked hard to put together a set of conditions which would anticipate all the Privy Council's objections. The proposed contract began in the usual way, with the promise to marry, but it then moved on to a series of clauses drastically limiting Philip's powers as Mary's consort. He would, of course, style himself King of England, and he would assist the Queen in the tasks of government, but 'saving always the kingdom's laws, privileges and customs.' He would relinquish all claim to dispose of offices, posts and benefices. These would be bestowed only upon Englishmen and all business would be conducted in 'the languages used of old in the kingdom, and by natives'. A royal bridegroom had probably never offered such self-imposed limitations before, but this was a highly unusual situation and Charles V knew that English fears about the Prince could easily ruin all his plans.

The rest of the contract followed more conventional lines. There were the customary arrangements for property. No official dowry was stated for, of course, Mary was bringing to the marriage her own kingdom. It was, however, specified that she would share in her husband's realms and dominions, and if he died first she would receive as a dower the sum of 60,000 Flemish pounds, two thirds coming from Spain and the rest from the Low Countries.

The eldest son of the marriage would succeed to his mother's throne and would also inherit Philip's lands in Lower Germany and Burgundy, but the kingdom of Spain was explicitly reserved for Don Carlos, the Prince's son by his first marriage, along with the right to various Italian territories. Only if Don Carlos died without children would these lands pass to the eldest child of Philip and Mary. After detailing the provision of suitable dowries for daughters of the marriage, the articles ended with the wish that 'there shall be whole-hearted and sincere fraternity, union and confederation between the

*Mary, Queen of Scots*, an engraving made to commemorate her marriage to the Dauphin Francis.
(Scottish National Portrait Gallery, Edinburgh)

Emperor, his heirs and dominions and the Queen and her dominions, which shall, God willing, endure forever'.

Presented with such favourable terms, Mary's representatives requested only very minor alterations, and on 12 January the articles were duly signed and sent back to the Emperor. On the face of it, everything seemed to be going very well. The Pope had already issued the dispensation necessary to allow Mary to marry her cousin's son, expressing delight as he did so. 'I believe he was never so much pleased about anything in his life,' said the imperial ambassador in Rome, describing how His Holiness's incredulity at Mary's accession had developed into a happy confidence that England would now return to the Roman Catholic fold. The Queen herself seemed full of shy eagerness to see her bridegroom, asking constantly when he would come and blushing and laughing self-consciously when the Lord Admiral and some of the other more daring courtiers teased her about the Prince.

Philip himself was not so enthusiastic. Sitting in his palace at Valladolid, poring over the copy of the articles sent to him, he was overcome with righteous indignation. Never had a king's powers been so publicly, so mortifyingly circumscribed. The sentences stating that he could not choose Spanish officials, and could not appoint whom he wished, were deeply insulting to him. He would grant power to his father's ambassadors to ratify the marriage treaty, of course, but at the same time he would protest against its terms. In the presence of the royal notary public, in company with the Duke of Alba, Ruy Gomez de Silva (his own chamberlain and close friend) and the Licenciate Minajaca, he swore a special oath.

He was not binding either himself or his heirs to observe the articles, he said, because by his own free will he had never agreed and never would agree to them. Indeed, he 'protested once, twice and thrice, or as many times as it was necessary to make the act legal' that although he ratified the terms in order that the marriage should take place, he was not bound by them. They were things done against his will, and only in order to attain the aforesaid object. Placing his right hand upon a cross drawn on the page, he swore this 'by Our Lord, Saint Mary, the sign of the cross and by the words of the Holy Gospel'.

This was not really an act of defiance against his father. The Duke of Alba and the Licenciate Minajaca were both members of Charles V's household, and it is almost certain that the Emperor knew about the oath in advance. Indeed, he may well have suggested it, and it seems possible that Mary knew about it too. The Prince's relationship with his father remained unaltered, and he was soon writing to tell him that Mary's acceptance of him was 'a source of satisfaction' to him, and he trusted that 'the result will contribute to the service of God and the welfare of Christendom'. He assured Charles that he would leave for England as soon as the proxy betrothal ceremonies had taken place, and in the meantime he was sending messengers to Galicia, Biscay and Andalusia to see how many vessels and provisions were available for the fleet he would take with him.

The articles safely signed, the Emperor and his advisers nevertheless remained nervous lest Philip's own attitude and the demeanour of his Spanish courtiers should endanger the match. Remembering how the Prince's offhand behaviour in the Low Countries had antagonised the German princes, they plied him with hints on his attitude towards his bride. 'For the love of God appear to be pleased,' wrote Don Juan Manrique de Lara from Rome, 'for there is nothing that could be of greater effect in the service of God or against the French.' 'Though I know it is not necessary,' said the Emperor, 'I will ask you to be especially careful, if God favours this match, to demonstrate much love and joy to the Queen and to do so both in public and private . . . and you will converse and be friendly with the English, behaving to them in a cordial manner.' Not to be left out, Simon Renard wrote frequently from London urging the Prince to write to Mary, send her a gift, and above all, come soon, for she would not marry in Lent. Moreover, his presence was desperately needed, for the Privy Councillors were unreliable and 'the Queen, being a woman, cannot penetrate their knavish tricks nor weigh matters of state'.

In fact, the danger lay not with the councillors but elsewhere. There was great public antipathy to the Spanish marriage, and for weeks past there had been alarming rumours of plotting. By the time the articles were signed, Mary and her council knew that traitors were scheming to depose her, marry Elizabeth to Edward Courtenay and put them on the throne instead. Finally, on 21 January, they managed to discover the details.

The Bishop of Winchester had become increasingly concerned about Courtenay, and he sent for him and questioned him closely. After a brief defiance, the young man broke down and told him everything. There was not just one plot: there were four. On Palm Sunday, 18 March 1554, Sir Thomas Wyatt would lead a rebellion in his native Kent and Sir Peter Carew, Sir James Crofts and the Duke of Suffolk would raise rebellions in the south-west of England, Herefordshire and the Midlands respectively. The French had promised their assistance too, albeit in vague terms.

The Bishop immediately altered his fellow councillors, minimising Courtenay's part as best he could, and even as he did so the rebels realised that their plot had been revealed. They could not possibly wait until Palm Sunday now. They would have to act at once. In the event, none of the conspirators except

Wyatt met with any success and within days Carew had fled to France and Suffolk had gone into hiding. The rebellion would centre on Kent.

The son of one of Henry VIII's favourite courtiers, Wyatt was an experienced soldier, motivated by a hatred of the Spanish match. He was at his castle of Allington when the news of the impending marriage was made public, and he offered at once to lead a rebellion. Marching to Maidstone with a growing number of supporters, he issued a proclamation urging everyone to help him to secure the 'liberty and commonwealth endangered by the Queen's intention of marrying a foreigner', and when a herald arrived from court to proclaim

102

him a traitor, he snatched the document from the man's hands before he could utter one word.

Soon he had fifteen hundred men with him, and he set up his headquarters in Rochester Castle. The Duke of Norfolk marched out from London to stop him but, when his soldiers began deserting in substantial numbers, the Duke fled, losing his artillery, his plate and all the money he had with him. Thus encouraged, Wyatt set out to march on the capital. On 29 January he made camp at Blackheath with some four thousand men.

The citizens of London panicked, the Privy Council argued and wrangled about what should be done and the Queen complained angrily to Lord Paget that, although her councillors had promised her a special bodyguard, they had not provided a single man. Falling to his knees, Paget protested that he had spent the past fortnight trying to raise troops, but as he had only one voice in the council, he could not do everything himself. Desperately worried in case the disturbances should threaten her coming marriage, Mary begged Charles V to send help.

Embroiled as he was in his perpetual war with France, the Emperor had neither men nor money to spare, and in any event his soldiers could not have arrived in England quickly enough. Mary therefore decided that she must place her trust in God and, when the Count of Egmont and Charles V's other special ambassadors went on 1 February to ask her permission to return home, they found her surprisingly calm. 'Though she had reason enough to be perplexed,' they noted, '[she] showed a firm spirit.' That same afternoon she set out in person to rally the Londoners to her defence.

Putting on her crown and her robes of state, she summoned her Privy Councillors, made sure that the contrite Edward Courtenay was with her, and went to the Guildhall to address the citizens. The hundreds of people who crowded round to hear her were much impressed. The Queen stood before them proudly and addressed them in her deep voice, with courage and resolution. Her aims were to administer justice, keep order and protect the

*London in the seventeenth century*, by an unknown artist of the Dutch school.
(Museum of London)

people's peace and tranquility, she told them. She was marrying because her Privy Council had asked her to do so, not out of some personal desire. If her subjects were really opposed to her marriage, then she would reconsider. The matter could be discussed properly in Parliament. Should they so wish, she would remain single, but in this moment of crisis they must stand by her. Provided they defended her against the rebels, she was 'minded to live and die with them, and strain every nerve in their cause, for this time their fortunes, goods, honour, personal safety, wives and children were in the balance'. If they bore themselves like good subjects, she would be bound to stand by them, for they would deserve the care of their sovereign lady.

Her words were greeted with a roar of approval. The crowd threw their caps into the air, and the following morning more than twenty thousand Londoners volunteered to stand against Wyatt. The Queen's speech had come not a moment too soon. Even as she spoke, Wyatt had been continuing his inexorable advance. Now, when he reached Southwark, he found that all the bridges in the vicinity had been destroyed to prevent him from crossing the Thames. He spent three days there, his soldiers looting the Chancellor's library in Winchester House, and then he moved on to Kingston, where he did manage to get over to the north bank.

The Bishop and several other Privy Councillors urged Mary to flee to the greater safety of Windsor, but she knew that, if she did, she would risk losing her crown. Strengthened by her new confidence as Philip's future wife, she decided to remain in London. On 7 February 1554, Wyatt arrived at Kensington and managed to slip past Pembroke's cavalry at Hyde Park Corner. Sir John Gage was waiting for him at Charing Cross with a group of young noblemen, one of whom was Edward Courtenay. As soon as the first blows were struck, Courtenay and the Earl of Worcester took to their heels, shouting

'All is lost!' and Wyatt tramped on, at the head of his now drastically dwindling force.

Finally, he arrived at Ludgate, to find the great city gate shut against him. Defiantly he hammered on it, shouting that the Queen was going to pardon him. 'Avaunt, traitor! Thou shalt not come in here!' bellowed Lord Admiral Howard, who was on the other side, and Wyatt fell back. Fighting still, he retreated to Temple Bar, but there he surrendered to Sir Maurice Berkeley. He was sent to the Tower, Sir James Crofts, the Duke of Suffolk and the other ringleaders were arrested, and the rebellion was over. Once again, Mary felt, she had been saved by a miracle.

*Sir John Gage*, Mary's Lord Chamberlain, by Holbein. (The Royal Collection © 1993 Her Majesty The Queen)

# 8

## THE RELUCTANT BRIDEGROOM

*AFTER THE* Duke of Northumberland's rising, Mary had been astonishingly merciful towards those who had tried to deprive her of the throne. This time, it was rather different. On 15 February 1554 she wrote to the Emperor telling him that the revolt had been crushed and adding, 'I trust, therefore, that the result will be to establish my reign more firmly than ever, to enable the alliance with my Lord the Prince to be concluded and to purify the kingdom by exemplary punishment inflicted on the guilty.'

Those she had pardoned before, those she had treated with generosity – Suffolk, Courtenay, Elizabeth – had betrayed her. She would not make the same mistake twice. The Emperor had been right. She must show severity to the rebels, and she would make sure that none of those who had wrongfully sought to usurp her throne could ever challenge her again. Only then would it be safe for Philip to come to England, and nothing was going to stand in the way of that.

Gallows were set up in Southwark, at Leadenhall, in Cheapside, Fleet Street, Charing Cross and at more than twenty other places in the city, and some of the prisoners were sent home to their Kentish villages to be hanged there. Even so, the Queen was not indiscriminate in her execution of the lesser rebels. In all, just over a hundred ordinary prisoners were hanged, but Mary pardoned four hundred more.

There could be no forgiveness for the principal persons involved, however. For months, she had been refusing to execute Lady Jane Grey and her husband, despite the fact that they had been condemned for treason. Now, she could hold out against her council's arguments no longer. While the young

Prayer book carried by Lady Jane Grey at her execution.
(By permission of the British Library)

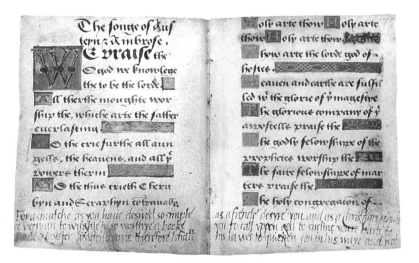

couple were alive, heretics and traitors would scheme to put them on the throne.

Lord Guildford Dudley went to the block first. Jane saw his body as they carried it into the chapel for burial, but she betrayed no emotion. When the Lieutenant of the Tower led her from her chamber, she seemed utterly calm. Dressed in the same gown she had worn at her trial, she carried a book in her hands and prayed as she went. Her two gentlewomen, walking behind her, wept inconsolably. She mounted the steps of the scaffold and faced the councillors and other officials who had assembled to see the death sentence carried out. She was innocent of any part in the conspiracies against the Queen, she said, and she added, 'I pray you all, good Christian people, to bear me witness that I die a true Christian woman . . . this plague or punishment is happily and worthily happened unto me for my sins.'

She knelt to say *Miserere mei Deus*, in English, as befitted a Protestant, then she stood up, handing her gloves and her handkerchief to one of her ladies, and giving her book to Sir John Bruges, the Lieutenant of the Tower. The executioner went to help her untie her gown, but she waved him away, asking her women to assist her instead. They took her cap and her neckerchief from her, and handed her a fine kerchief to bind round her eyes.

When the executioner knelt to ask her forgiveness and told her to stand upon the straw strewn on the scaffold, she saw the block for the first time. 'I pray you dispatch me quickly!' she exclaimed. She tied the kerchief round her own eyes, and then groped among the straw for the block, crying out in dismay, 'What shall I do? Where is it?' One of the bystanders guided her towards it, and she lay down. 'Lord into thy hands I commend my spirit!' she said loudly, and the axe fell.

That same day, Edward Courtenay was imprisoned in the Tower and Elizabeth set out for London, under deep suspicion. When she had first been summoned to court at the beginning of the rising, she had sent word that illness prevented her from obeying. As soon as the rebellion was over, Mary dispatched two of the royal doctors to see her. They reported that she was still unwell, but she was fit to travel by litter, provided she took the journey slowly. She was accordingly brought to the capital, dressed all in white, pale and defiant. She was lodged in apartments in the Palace of Whitehall as far away from the rest of the court as possible, and the Queen refused to see her.

Mary was almost certain that her sister had been involved in Wyatt's conspiracy, and Elizabeth's enemies on the Privy Council were determinedly trying to find conclusive evidence that she had been implicated. They did not succeed, and for a month the Queen and the council tried to decide what should be done with her. Meanwhile, Wyatt was tried for treason and on 15 March he was sentenced to death. Two days later, Elizabeth was told that she was being taken to the Tower. Terrified, she wrote the Queen an agitated letter protesting her innocence and begging for an audience.

When she read it, Mary was deeply upset. She had probably kept Elizabeth away for fear that she would weaken should she see the girl. Now, the sight of her sister's writing brought all her ambivalent feelings surging back and she turned furiously on the two councillors who had brought her the message, telling them that they should never have agreed to Elizabeth's request. They would not have dared to act thus in her father's time, she cried, and 'only wished he might come to life again for a month'. The following morning, Elizabeth was taken by barge to the Tower.

Trinity College Chapel, Cambridge, built by Mary after Wyatt's rebellion had been crushed. (The Master and Fellows of Trinity College, Cambridge: photograph, L R Goodey)

The full details of Wyatt's rebellion had been kept from Prince Philip, lest he be further discouraged from coming to England but, although the danger was past now, Mary had not yet received a single letter from him and she was becoming increasingly distressed. Time and again she told Renard, with tears in her eyes, that she would rather die than let any harm come to the Prince, she sent assurances that she would 'fulfil towards him all the duties which ladies were bound to discharge where their husbands are concerned', and she was full of helpful advice, urging him to bring his own trustworthy physicians and cooks.

Philip had thought of that already. Indeed, he intended to bring with him three thousand members of his court, fifteen hundred mules and other beasts of burden, and sixty ships. This vast retinue took time to assemble and although the vessels had begun to gather at La Coruña at the beginning of February, heavy rains had made it difficult to get in supplies. Urged on by constant orders from Charles V to make haste, he finally abandoned the notion of taking so many courtiers with him, and said that he would set off as soon as enough ships were ready to transport himself, his household and his servants. He also promised to take no more servants than he really needed, for he realised that, once in England, he would have 'to accept the services of natives, in order to show them that I mean to trust myself to them and favour them as if I were an Englishman born'.

In the meantime, Mary had to console herself with the proxy betrothal. The Count of Egmont arrived back in London bearing a magnificent ring from Charles V, and the ceremony was held with some splendour on 8 March. The Queen and the Count, acting for Philip, exchanged promises to marry, before the entire Privy Council, with the Bishop of Winchester officiating and the Holy Sacrament placed on an altar in the room.

Kneeling, Mary reiterated her assertion that she was agreeing to marry not out of any carnal affection or desire, nor for any motive whatsoever except her

*Venus and Adonis*, commissioned by Philip from Titian, and sent to London on the occasion of his marriage.

*Below. Mary blessing cramp rings on Good Friday*, about 1555.
(Westminster Cathedral Library)

kingdom's honour and prosperity, and the repose and tranquillity of her subjects. She begged those present to pray that God would give her the grace to accomplish the marriage and then favour the union. At that, the Count produced the ring and Mary expressed astonished delight. Although it had not come from Philip himself, she showed it proudly to everyone there.

She then presented the Count with a gift of jewellery and sent him on his way to Spain, to tell the Prince that the betrothal had taken place. He should be able to set out at once, she hoped. Anxious to show her gratitude to the Emperor, she sent him a special gift too. When Good Friday came, she revived the traditional ceremony of blessing rings which were then believed to give relief from cramp and other ailments. She selected more than a hundred and fifty of them for Charles himself, with additional bundles for his sisters. The Bishop of Arras, entrusted with the task of distributing them, received them with some scepticism. It was good of Mary to send them, he told his friend Renard, and he only hoped that, 'they will prove more efficacious than those blessed by some of her predecessors'.

Charles was in the meantime doing all he could to make sure that there were no untoward scenes when his son did arrive in England. Spaniards had a reputation for arrogance, and the English were strange people. Philip must make sure that his entourage consisted of 'tactful, moderate and courteous men who shall be told to put up with anything from the English in order to win popularity'.

There were alarming rumours that the Prince intended taking with him a contingent of Roman Catholic theologians, despite all his father's warnings that religious matters must be taken slowly, and reports that the Spanish grandees were to be accompanied by their wives were almost as bad: the presence of these ladies would give rise to all manner of difficulties. When he heard that Philip was thinking of calling on him in Brussels *en route* for London, he immediately forbade him to do any such thing. Mary would be disappointed if her fiancé did not go to her at the earliest possible moment, and she 'does not deserve that'. By the beginning of April Charles was desperately instructing Alba, 'Duke, for the love of God see to it that my son behaves in the right manner, for otherwise I tell you I would rather never have taken the matter in hand at all.'

Determined that the wedding should take place as quickly as possible, Mary opened her second Parliament on 6 April so that the members could approve the marriage contract. They did so, but the religious legislation that she and the Chancellor had hoped to introduce was blocked by the House of Lords. The Queen's intention was to reintroduce the acts against heresy which would, for example, permit the burning of Protestants, but Lord Paget, Lord Rich and an influential group of peers were afraid that this was a preliminary to the Chancellor forcibly taking back the Church lands iñ their possession, and they refused to pass the act.

Parliament rose in a state of disarray at the beginning of May. The Privy Council was as deeply divided as ever between Roman Catholics and Protestants, the Chancellor and Lord Paget were scarcely on speaking terms, all were jealous of Simon Renard's influence with the Queen, and she seemed powerless to remedy the situation. 'What one does, another undoes, that one advises, another opposes,' said Renard, while Mary herself complained bitterly that she spent all her days in shouting at her council, but with no result. If only Philip would come, all her problems would be solved.

*Joanna, Princess of Portugal,*
Philip's sister, who ruled Spain
as his regent, by Mor.

Apparently under the impression that he was doing his best, the Prince continued to move with his usual stately, infuriating calm. On 1 April his younger sister, the recently widowed Joanna, Princess of Portugal, was appointed to be Regent of Spain in his absence, and at the beginning of May he sent most of his household ahead to La Coruña. A group of English noblemen arrived to escort him to his new kingdom but he could not leave, of course, until his sister arrived from Portugal. However, he had at least decided to send his bride a gift. A beautiful and costly diamond set in a rose, which had once been given by his father to his mother, was now entrusted to the Marquis de Las Navas to take to Mary. Edward, Lord Dudley, one of the group of visiting dignitaries, offered to escort him to London, and wrote home approvingly that the Marquis was a most suitable person for the mission: 'He is an ancient gentleman about the year of fifty or better, bearing himself very honourably.'

While he waited for his sister's arrival, Philip went to see his grandmother, Joanna the Mad, who was still alive and living in seclusion, then his sister was delayed by a fever and so he set off on a tour of his favourite properties, visiting the forests of Segovia, inspecting the Prado, seeing the building work

*The Emperor Maximilian II* and his wife, Philip's sister, Maria, by
G Arcimboldo. Their eldest daughter eventually became Philip's
fourth wife.
(Kunsthistorisches Museum, Vienna)

he had ordered to be done at Toledo and poring over the latest letter from
Titian, offering him three new paintings. He spent as much time as possible in
the company of his young son, Don Carlos, and he presumably took a reluctant
farewell from his mistress, Doña Isabel, who was to be consigned to a convent.

Fretting and looking constantly for news of his arrival, Mary was encouraged by the appearance in May of two more officials from Charles V, charged
with the task of making regulations to ensure that Philip's Spaniards and the
English courtiers agreed. They moved on almost at once to Southampton, to be
ready for his arrival. Meanwhile, Philip's English household was already
being appointed. The Earl of Arundel would be Lord Steward for both the
King and Queen, and under his supervision would be three hundred and fifty
attendants and servants of every degree.

However much Mary's nobility might dislike the notion of the marriage,
they were eager for places for themselves and their sons. Seven peers,
including the Duke of Norfolk, would be Gentlemen of Philip's Chamber, the
Lord Admiral's son was to be one of the cupbearers, Sir Robert Rochester
would be Controller and of course there would be a full complement of lesser
men, including the pages who would tend the fires, yeomen of the laundry,

grooms of the scullery, clerks of the spicery and nightwatchmen. In mid-June, they all set off for Southampton to wait for their new master.

At long last, it seemed to Mary that her bridegroom's arrival was really imminent. Her spirits rose and she even felt more kindly disposed towards her sister. Monsieur de Noailles reported that she had hung Elizabeth's portrait in her gallery again, having taken it down during the Wyatt rebellion, and she was heard to mention her by name once more. By the middle of May, she had even relented sufficiently to have her sister transferred from the Tower to the much less frightening castle of Woodstock in Oxfordshire.

Anxious discussions about Elizabeth's future continued. It was said that Mary was considering marrying her to some safe supporter of the Emperor, and for a few weeks she thought of sending Elizabeth to stay with the Queen Dowager. The latter was willing to have the girl with her, although she pointed out that their personalities might clash, but in the end nothing came of the idea. As June began, Mary was far more taken up with her own marriage and, when the Marquis de Las Navas finally arrived with her diamond, she hurried off to Guildford to meet him. From there she moved to Farnham, desperately impatient at the lack of news from Spain and anxious about reports that the supplies for her future husband's household were rapidly running out.

July came, and there was still no sign of the Prince, but by this time he had in fact met his sister at Alcantara. They had travelled together for two or three days so that he could instruct her on her future role, then she had left for Valladolid. At Santiago de Compostela he had finally encountered the English ambassadors and ratified the marriage articles. On 27 June he had arrived at La Coruña, where he found his entire fleet anchored and supplies being put on board. He embarked on 12 July, and that same evening he set sail for England.

Mary spent almost three weeks at the Bishop of Winchester's castle at Farnham before moving on to the medieval moated palace at Bishop's

Farnham Castle, where Mary stayed on her way to Winchester.
(English Heritage)

Waltham, a few miles from Southampton. One of the greatest ecclesiastical residences in England, it had formerly been another of the Bishop's houses, but during Edward VI's reign it had been taken from him and it now belonged to the Earl of Wiltshire. In its spacious apartments, she waited impatiently until at long last, on 19 July, came the news that Philip's fleet had been sighted off the Isle of Wight.

The Lord Admiral, who had been cruising to and fro for the past three months, met the Prince at the Needles and escorted him to Southampton. Next morning, the Marquis de Las Navas and a group of young English noblemen were among the first to go out to the royal vessel, followed by the official welcoming party, consisting of the Earl of Arundel and several senior Privy Councillors, in a richly gilded and decorated barge. The Earl had been entrusted with a special mission, and as soon as he was presented he invested the Prince with the Order of the Garter, fastening round his leg a costly band of diamonds, rubies and pearls.

After dinner, Philip and his party were rowed to the shore. He was startled to find awaiting him not only the expected bodyguard of a hundred royal archers in his own livery, but a host of other eager gentlemen. These, it was explained, were his English household. Philip was horrified. He had brought all his own people with him: two dukes, five marquises, six counts, the Admiral of Castile, the Bishop of Cuenca, chaplains, doctors, grooms, cooks and pages. How could he possibly make use of them all, let alone pay them?

He had no time to worry about that particular problem, for as the town's artillery boomed a salute and the Queen's minstrels played, Don Juan de Figueroa, an emissary from his father, stepped forward with an important message from the Emperor. Charles V was resigning to Philip his own title of

*Sir Anthony Browne,* Philip's Master of the Horse, by Eworth, 1569. (National Portrait Gallery, London)

King of Naples, so that his son could go to his wedding as a monarch, not a mere Prince. Deciding that he had better wait until he had told Mary the pleasing news before announcing it publicly, Philip turned his attention to Sir Anthony Browne, his English Master of the Horse, who was kneeling before him to make a loyal address, in Latin. Sir Anthony then helped him to mount the beautifully caparisoned white horse which was to take him to the nearest church, so that he could give thanks for his safe arrival. Off he rode, with his two households tramping along on foot behind him, glaring at each other suspiciously.

Since his unfortunate experience in the Netherlands, Philip had learned tact, and as soon as the service was over and he was safely installed in his lodgings, he made a gracious speech, in Latin, assuring his English hearers that he did not come to their country as a stranger or foreigner intent on increasing his own power and wealth. On the contrary, God had sent him there to marry the Queen, and as long as the English were faithful subjects, he would be their good Prince. This was well received, and at the lavish banquet afterwards he completed the good impression he had made by seizing a cup of English beer and downing it with apparent relish. His Spanish courtiers must henceforth forget all their own customs and live like Englishmen, he told them.

He woke next morning to torrential rain and decided to spend a day or two in Southampton recovering from the journey. He was always a bad sailor and he had been dreadfully sick. Moreover, the ships carrying his lesser servants, his horses and his baggage had gone to the larger harbour at Portsmouth and they had not yet joined him. That day, he received the Bishop of Winchester and said all the right things when his visitor handed him a diamond ring from the Queen. Realising that he was expected to return the compliment, he hastily dispatched Ruy Gomez, his favourite courtier, with a ring for Mary.

On Monday 23 July, in pouring rain, he set off for Winchester, where the marriage was to take place. It was six o'clock in the evening when his procession entered the city. Mounted on his white horse, he was an impressive figure in his gold-embroidered cloak with matching doublet and hose, a fine white feather in his gold-embroidered hat. He went first to the cathedral to attend a *Te Deum* and then he was taken by torchlight to the Dean's house, where he was to stay. Mary had also arrived, and she was lodging in the Bishop's Palace. Having changed his wet clothes and eaten a quiet supper, he went out at ten o'clock that evening to walk the short distance through the gardens to the palace. The moment he and Mary had so long been anticipating, with varying degrees of apprehension, had come at last.

Writing a description of the Queen just three weeks later, a former Venetian ambassador in England described her as being 'of low stature, with a red and white complexion and very thin'. Her eyes were light-coloured, her hair reddish and her nose rather low and wide, he said, but 'Were not her age on the decline she might be called beautiful rather than the contrary' and her expression indicated a 'great benignity and clemency'. For her first encounter with her future husband, she had dressed with great care, putting on a black velvet gown over a silver petticoat, and as usual she was wearing magnificent jewels including, presumably, the diamond he had sent her.

When she knew that Philip was in the palace, she hurried excitedly to the door of her chamber, her ladies and several of her councillors crowding behind her. There was a moment's pause, the sound of feet on the back stairs and then there he was, her bridegroom, a slim, erect young man with yellow hair, a

Bishop's Waltham Palace.
(English Heritage)

yellow beard and grey eyes like her own. Smiling, he kissed her, took her by
the hand and led her to a seat in her Presence Chamber in the West Hall. Soon
they were happily engrossed in conversation, she talking to him eagerly, he
answering with kindly courtesy. Her ladies looked at each other in relief. Their
mistress liked him. It was going to be all right.

No one has decided which language Mary and Philip used to each other. She
certainly understood Spanish but she was said not to speak it, and when the
Duchess of Alba arrived a few days later the Queen employed the services of
the Marquis de Las Navas as interpreter. She used no such intermediary even
in her first conversation with Philip, and it may be that they spoke in Latin.
Both were fluent in it and well accustomed to conducting business with
foreign emissaries in that tongue.

They spoke to each other for quite some time, until it grew late, and Philip

Wolvesey, the Bishop's Palace in Winchester, scene of Mary's first meeting with Philip.
(English Heritage)

*Mary I*, wearing the diamond and the famous pearl, 'La Peregrina', which Philip gave her.
The portrait was painted by Mor in 1554.

had to return to his lodgings. Before he did so, however, he asked Mary to teach him a few words in English to say to her councillors. Delighted, she whispered a reply. He stood up to take his leave, and as he passed the gentlemen he enunciated with care, 'Good night, my lords all.'

It was an excellent beginning. Next morning she sent him a gift of two sumptuous outfits to wear on his wedding day, and in the afternoon they met again, in public, in the great East Hall of the Bishop's Palace, to discuss the final arrangements. They had chosen 25 July to marry, for it was the feast of St James, Spain's patron saint. Philip made his way to the cathedral at ten in the morning, to wait for his bride in a side chapel.

Mary arrived half an hour later, in a long procession of clergy, councillors and ladies. Before her walked her sword- and mace-bearers, and immediately behind her the Marchioness of Winchester and Sir John Gage carried the train of her elaborate golden robe. Slowly she mounted the platform erected in the cathedral for the ceremony, and Philip appeared at her side. He was wearing one of the outfits she had sent him, a matching gold robe lined with crimson satin and trimmed with crimson velvet, the sleeves sewn with pearl buttons.

Together they stepped up onto a purple-draped dais, the Queen's choristers and the cathedral choir sang, and the organ played. The bridegroom, an ardent lover of music, presumably appreciated the glorious singing which so impressed the congregation, but the Queen appeared oblivious to almost everything around her. Her eyes were fixed on the Holy Sacrament on the altar, and throughout the ensuing ceremony she looked neither to right nor to left.

Don Juan de Figueroa read out the Latin deed conferring the kingdom of Naples upon Philip, then the Bishop of Winchester made an address in English, explaining that the Queen was marrying with the consent of Parliament, for the good of her realm. Moving over to the royal couple, he began the marriage service. When he asked who gave the Queen away, the Marquis of Winchester, the Earl of Derby, the Earl of Bedford and the Earl of Pembroke stepped forward together. She had no near male relative in the country, and so these representative Privy Councillors performed the role usually assigned to a father.

A simple gold band was placed upon her finger, unlike the usual gem-set

*William Paulet, 1st Marquis of Winchester*, by an unknown artist. (National Portrait Gallery, London)

Oak chair, traditionally said to have been used by Mary at her wedding. (By courtesy of the Dean and Chapter of Winchester Cathedral: photograph, John Crook)

wedding rings of the time and very different from Mary's other jewellery. She had asked for the plain ring specially, it seems, 'because maidens were so married in old times'. Nuptial Mass was celebrated, and then Garter King of Arms proclaimed their majesties' new style: 'Philip and Mary, by the grace of God, King and Queen of England, France and Naples, Jerusalem and Ireland, defenders of the faith, Princes of Spain and Sicily, Archdukes of Austria, Dukes of Milan, Burgundy and Brabant, Counts of Habsburg, Flanders and the Tyrol.'

Fanfares sounded, and the King and Queen walked slowly from the cathedral, hand in hand beneath a canopy of state. Through cheering crowds they went, to the Bishop's Palace and up to the East Hall which had been hung with cloth-of-gold and silk. There the wedding banquet was held, with Mary and Philip sitting at the high table with the Bishop, eating from gold and silver dishes. Mary had intended her husband to wear his second new outfit for this part of the day, a cloth-of-gold robe lined with purple satin, embroidered with roses and pomegranates and sewn with gold beads, seed pearls and diamond buttons. However, as he himself noted later, when he gazed upon its splendour, 'it seemed to me too ornate', and so he had changed into one of his own more sober suits. If Mary was disappointed, her regrets were soon forgotten as they laughed and talked together, and then adjourned to one of the other great halls in the palace to join in the dancing.

They took supper separately, in their own chambers, and the evening ended with the ancient ceremony of blessing the nuptial bed. The Bishop of Winchester and his colleagues said the traditional prayers, the courtiers watched and joked, and then everyone went away, leaving Mary and her husband alone. Inexperienced and, as she had so often said, never interested in sexual love, Mary lay down with Philip that night from determination and a sense of duty rather than in the expectation of enjoying their physical relationship. God, who had performed so many miracles for her already, would surely send her the son she needed, and she was resolved to do her part.

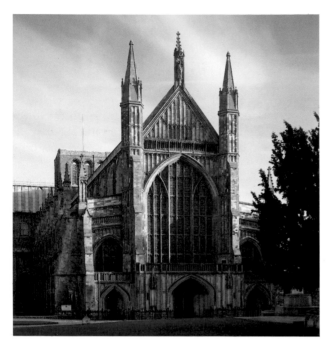

Winchester Cathedral,
the west front.
(By courtesy of the Dean
and Chapter of
Winchester Cathedral:
photograph,
A F Kersting)

Winchester Cathedral,
the high altar.
(By courtesy of the Dean
and Chapter of
Winchester Cathedral:
photograph,
A F Kersting)

# 9

## *THE HAPPY BRIDE*

*N*EXT MORNING, custom dictated that Mary should remain in seclusion with her ladies, so she spent some time composing a grateful note to the Emperor, thanking him 'for allying me with a Prince so full of virtues that the realm's honour and tranquillity will certainly be thereby increased, assuring you that I will take pains to serve you in gratitude'. Up at seven that first morning, Philip went to Mass twice that day and gave every appearance of being content. He was anxious to move on to Brussels, for he had ambitions to take part in his first military campaign against the French, but he could

*Mary touching for the King's Evil*, to cure sufferers of scrofula.
(Westminster Cathedral Library)

console himself with the thought that his stay in England would be of short duration. He had tactfully kept from his wife the news that his father wanted him to travel to the Low Countries in a week's time, and before he had time to break the news to her, Charles changed his mind. Philip should stay where he was for the time being, concentrating on bringing his new subjects back to the Church of Rome.

If he had reservations about his bride, Philip kept them to himself. This marriage was far too important to be jeopardised by any personal feelings. Everyone knew what a devout and good woman Mary was. His father was constantly reminding him that the wedding would never have been arranged at all if it had not been for her persistence. Her fidelity to her religion and to the Emperor's cause throughout all her past troubles made her someone to be treated with gratitude and consideration, and her almost pathetic eagerness to please made it simple enough for him to do that. The widower of the Portuguese Infanta and the longtime partner of Doña Isabel knew how to satisfy a woman, even if he did not find her attractive.

As for Mary, Philip's very presence brought her an overwhelming sense of relief. For so much of her life she had felt alone, isolated among her enemies, and ever since her accession she had been struggling with these councillors of hers, none of whom she could trust. Now, at last, she had a true friend, someone who shared her dearest ambitions, someone whose masculine authority would make her task of ruling the country so much easier. The fact that he was a close relative, a pleasing companion and even more handsome than his portrait had suggested made her happiness complete. Soon her husband was arousing in her emotions she had never thought to feel.

Ruy Gomez wrote to tell his friend Francisco de Eraso, the Emperor's principal secretary, 'Our marriage has gone off admirably. The Queen is a very good creature, though rather older than we had been told. But his Highness is so tactful and attentive to her that I am sure they will be very happy, and Our Lord will do the rest.' 'The royal couple', said Simon Renard, 'are bound together by such deep love that the marriage may be expected to be a perfect union.'

Despite the restrictions placed on him by his marriage contract, Philip was soon involving himself in affairs of state. The first week of the marriage was spent in Winchester, but already he was attending Mass, dining in public, seeing Privy Councillors, poring over state papers and every day discovering new problems. He tried to solve the difficulty of his two households by allowing both his Spanish and his English noblemen to attend him, but when the English realised that they were consigned to the periphery, while his own gentlemen performed the more personal tasks, they were soon seething with resentment. Worse than that, he could see for himself how cumbersome and divided was the English Privy Council, as Mary's lords came to him one by one to complain about their colleagues and hint that they themselves ought to be rewarded for their support of Charles V. Moreover, he was horrified to discover how short of money Mary was. Loans would have to be arranged from Spain and the Low Countries as soon as possible. Putting his wife's realm in order would be no easy task.

Despite her husband's assiduous hard work, Mary was still almost constantly occupied with the cares of government, rising at dawn for prayers and Mass before transacting business 'incessantly, often until after midnight', scarcely stopping to eat. On certain days she dined in public with her husband, and she liked to play the lute and the spinet, but she was always short of time, for she could not delegate, and recently she had been suffering from headaches as well as the troublesome palpitations which had always plagued her. Medicine and frequent bloodlettings did not seem to help; indeed, they must have had a weakening effect. It was evident to her husband and his own advisers that she did not have a real hold over her councillors, and Gomez was soon commenting, 'The Queen is a good soul, but not as able as we were led to suppose – I mean as a stateswoman.'

She did allow herself a little leisure to admire the gifts and the letters of congratulation on her wedding, and she was particularly pleased with a fine parcel of dresses and caps from Philip's sister, Joanna. 'I believe', said Gomez, 'that if she dressed in our fashions she would not look so old and flabby.' His early optimism about the marriage had faded fast, and only two days after his first letter to his friend Eraso he was telling him, 'To speak frankly with you, it will take a great God to drink this cup . . . the best of it is that the King fully realises that the marriage was concluded for no fleshly considerations, but in order to remedy the disorders of this kingdom and preserve the Low Countries.' The Queen, said another of the Spaniards, 'is a perfect saint, and dresses badly.'

Mercifully ignorant of their contempt, Mary set off with her husband for London, pausing at Windsor on the way so that Philip could be installed as Sovereign of the Order of the Garter. She gave him a handsome jewel-encrusted dagger to mark the occasion, and it was she who also provided the purple velvet mantle with its long train which was placed about his shoulders during the ceremony in St George's Chapel. Apparently feeling that it, too, was a trifle ostentatious, Philip later ordered his own Garter robes with no train at all.

No doubt as a result of the appalling weather, the King and Queen were both suffering from heavy colds, and they decided to stay at Windsor for a few days. Observing them closely, Simon Renard thought that their happiness made it 'a great pleasure to see them together' and he assured the Emperor that Philip was 'altogether changed from what he was when he last left the Low Countries'. Ruy Gomez was still attributing the success of the marriage entirely to Philip. 'He treats the Queen very kindly,' he reported, 'and well knows how to pass over the fact that she is no good from the point of view of fleshly sensuality. He makes her so happy that the other day when they were alone she almost talked love-talk with him, and he replied in the same vein.' As for Mary herself, she was, she told the Emperor, 'happier than I can say, and daily discover in the King, my husband and your son, so many virtues and perfections that I constantly pray God to grant me grace to please him and behave in all things as befits one who is so deeply embounden to him.'

Soon afterwards they set out for London, stopping at Richmond Palace for a day or two, then sailing down the Thames to Southwark in two separate royal barges. They landed at St Mary Overy, now Southwark Cathedral, and went into the Bishop of Winchester's town house next door for refreshments. After a few hours' hunting in Suffolk Park, they returned to Winchester House to spend the night and the next afternoon they crossed the Thames by bridge and made their ceremonial entry into the capital.

Most of Philip's Spanish attendants had sought permission to join Charles V's army and had gone off to Dover to make the Channel crossing. Without the presence of these arrogant strangers, the King was all the more enthusiastically

St George's Chapel, Windsor, from the west.
(By courtesy of the Dean and Chapter of St George's Chapel: photograph,
A F Kersting)

The Sovereign's Stall, St
George's Chapel,
Windsor.
(By courtesy of the Dean
and Chapter of St
George's Chapel:
photograph,
A F Kersting)

Southwark Cathedral, the high altar with Bishop Fox's screen. (By courtesy of the Dean and Chapter of Southwark Cathedral: photograph, Jarrold Publishing)

Map of London in the sixteenth century, by Georg Braun and Frans Hogenberg. (His Grace the Archbishop of Canterbury and the Trustees of Lambeth Palace Library)

received as he and Mary acknowledged the cheers, admired the decorations and watched the well-rehearsed pageants. There was one awkward moment when the Bishop of Winchester noticed a portrait of Henry VIII presenting Edward VI with a book inscribed 'The Word of God'. Furious at this apparently Protestant allusion, the Bishop summoned the unfortunate artist and threatened him with dire penalties unless he changed the picture. The man hastily painted out the book and replaced it with a pair of gloves.

Philip and Mary were probably unaware of this little contretemps as they marvelled at the imitation man on horseback who turned right round at their approach, admired three famous Philips from history adorning a scaffolding beside the stocks at Cornhill and gazed with delight as Orpheus played his harp on an artificial mountain while children attired as lions, wolves, bears and apes emerged from the undergrowth and pranced about in time to the music.

As usual, the *pièce de résistance* came at St Paul's Cathedral, where, from the top of the spire, 'a fellow came slipping upon a cord, as an arrow out of a bow ... to the ground, and lighted with his head on a great sort of feather bed' before clambering back up again to perform various other breathtaking feats. Installed that night in their Palace of Whitehall, Philip and Mary could look back on a most satisfactory day, as well as admiring two particularly fine wedding presents which had arrived from the Continent: a set of gold- and silver-embroidered tapestries from the Emperor, depicting his own victory against the Turks, and a gold and silver organ set with jewels, from the Queen of Poland.

*Cardinal Reginald Pole,* attributed to Sebastiano del Piombo. (His Grace the Archbishop of Canterbury: photograph, Courtauld Institute of Art, London)

Despite the premature return of his sullen Spaniards, blown back by contrary winds, Philip soon began to feel that he was making real progress in his attempts to improve the government of England, and the end of September brought news which would surely solve all their problems at a stroke. One of the royal doctors announced that the Queen was pregnant. At first it seemed too good to be true, and Mary herself could hardly believe it. Tremulous with delight, she allowed her ladies and her physicians to convince her that she had all the appropriate symptoms: nausea, swelling of the abdomen and heaviness of the breasts. It seemed that God was about to send her another miracle, a son to secure the Roman Catholic succession.

By the beginning of October even Philip was confident enough to lead her out in a celebratory dance in the Ladies Hall and send a message to his father announcing the happy news. The Emperor was overjoyed. Apart from his genuine pleasure on Mary's behalf he knew that, with the future of England safe, he could at last abdicate in favour of his son and retire to the Spanish monastery where he had long ago decided to spend his last years.

Cardinal Pole was equally pleased, and he sent a long letter telling Mary how delighted he had been to hear that 'His Divine Majesty had granted the Queen the grace of conceiving fruit in her corporeal womb.' The Cardinal was about to return to England for the first time since his banishment. His appointment as papal legate should have meant that he would travel to London at once, to carry out his mission of reconciling the English with Rome, but various factors had delayed his homecoming. Because he had been condemned as a traitor by Parliament in Henry VIII's reign, he could not safely return until the sentence had been lifted. Moreover, the Pope had also appointed him to negotiate a peace between the King of France and the Emperor, and he spent some months vainly travelling between Paris and Brussels in an attempt to reconcile the two old enemies.

In so doing he antagonised Charles, and the Emperor was in any case determined to delay Pole's journey to England for as long as possible. At first he had been afraid that the Cardinal might be a suitor for Mary's hand. (Pole was not actually an ordained priest, for all his high ecclesiastical office.) Even when that danger passed and the Queen was safely married to Philip, the Emperor was reluctant to let him travel to London. He could see how anxious Pole was to reconcile England with Rome, and he feared that, like Mary, the Cardinal might act too hastily. If he started demanding that the nobility hand over their Church lands, for instance, he could ruin everything. The result was that Pole was still fulminating in Brussels, sending long and vehement letters of complaint not only to Mary but also to her husband.

Philip received one letter reminding him that, 'A year has passed since I began to knock at the door of this royal house, and none has opened to me. King, if you ask, as those are wont to do, who hear a knock at the door, "Who is there?" I will reply, "Is it I, who rather than consent that this house should be closed to her who now possesses it [Mary] with you, preferred banishment and twenty years of exile . . . " ' Knowing that only Pole could grant the English the absolution necessary before they could be reconciled with Rome, Philip decided that the time had come to allow the Cardinal to cross to England. He sent Renard to confer with the Emperor and Pole, the Pope was persuaded to agree that it would be better 'to abandon all Church property rather than risk the shipwreck of the operation' and Charles V at last agreed that the Cardinal could return.

The shrine of St Edward the Confessor in Westminster Abbey, restored
on Mary's orders in 1556.
(By courtesy of the Dean and Chapter of Westminster Abbey)

In the meantime, the King and Queen went to Westminster on 12 November
1554 to open Parliament, each arrayed in crimson velvet trimmed with ermine.
Mary was in an open litter, as befitted her condition, and Philip on horseback
drew many an admiring comment, if one of his Spanish friends is to be
believed. All around them, he said, were exclamations of, 'Oh, how handsome
the King is!', 'Oh, how kind and gentle he looks', and 'Oh, what a good
husband he is! How honourably and lovingly he treats the Queen!' Mary
herself seemed in excellent health. Her dresses no longer fitted her and,
according to Luis Varegas, one of Philip's retinue, 'She is fatter and has a
better colour than when she was married, a sign that she is happy, and indeed
she is said to be very happy. The King also is.'

Parliament obediently repealed the legislation banishing the Cardinal, who
by now had set out for Calais. He was so delicate that he dared not risk riding,
and he had to be carried in a litter, very slowly, a few miles a day. He
eventually arrived at Dover and was honourably escorted to Gravesend, to sail
up the river by royal barge. When he disembarked at Whitehall, Philip was

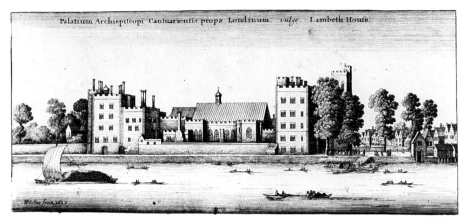

*Lambeth Palace*, engraved by W Hollar in the seventeenth century.
(His Grace the Archbishop of Canterbury and the Trustees of Lambeth Palace Library)

having dinner, but he hurried down to greet the visitor, his cap in hand as a sign of respect. A thin, ascetic figure with a spiritual expression and a heavy beard, the Cardinal spoke to him enthusiastically and then they went upstairs to the Long Gallery where Mary was waiting.

She curtsied deeply when she saw them and, when the Cardinal knelt before her, both she and Philip hastily helped him to his feet. As she did so, she drew in her breath sharply. She had felt the babe leap in her womb, she explained, whereupon the Cardinal smiled and quoted in Latin, 'Blessed among women, and blessed be the fruit of your womb.' They talked together in the Presence Chamber for more than half an hour, before Pole left to sail across the river to Lambeth Palace, where he would stay, since the Archbishop of Canterbury was still in prison, and his residence was therefore available.

The following Wednesday, they went to the Great Hall at Westminster, where the Lords and Commons had gathered. Philip and Mary took their places on the dais, beneath their royal canopy, and the Cardinal seated himself on a high-backed chair near the Queen. The Lord Chancellor spoke first, introducing the visitor. 'My lords of the Upper House and you masters of the

Electrotype medal of Philip II of Spain, after Jacopo da Trezzo, 1555.
(National Portrait Gallery, London)

Electrotype medal of Mary I, after Jacopo da Trezzo, about 1555.
(National Portrait Gallery, London)

The Great Hall,
Westminster.
(Royal Commission on
the Historical
Monuments of England)

Nether House', he began, 'here is present the right reverend father in God, my Lord Cardinal Pole, come from the Apostolic See of Rome as ambassador to the King and Queen's Majesty upon one of the most weightiest causes that ever happened in this realm . . .'

With that, Pole began to speak, extempore, with no hint of his usual hesitant, almost timid manner. Fluently and confidently he thanked them for receiving him, rehearsed England's long history as a Christian nation, and praised the Queen's constancy in religious matters. 'Being a virgin, helpless, naked and unarmed', she had nevertheless 'prevailed and had the victory over tyrants'. Now she was married to a mighty prince, and God would undoubtedly give them children.

After further praise of Charles V, the Cardinal turned to his own task. 'My commission is not of prejudice to any person,' he assured his hearers. 'I come not to destroy but to build. I come to reconcile, not to condemn. I come not to compel but to call again. I am not come to call anything in question already done, but my commission is of grace and clemency to such as will receive it, for touching all matters that be past, they shall be as things cast into the sea of forgetfulness.' He would therefore ask them to repeal all the legislation which stood in the way of their return to Rome.

Two days later, they went back to Westminster to hear Parliament's answer. It was a dull afternoon, and the great chamber was lit by torches. When they were all in position, the members presented a supplication to the King and Queen. They were, they said, 'very sorry and repentant of the schism and disobedience committed in this realm and the dominions of the same against the said See Apostolic'.

They would do all they could to repeal the offending laws, and they asked

Philip and Mary to intercede with the Cardinal, requesting that he might grant them absolution and receive them as repentant children 'into the bosom and unity of Christ's Church'. The entire company, apart from Philip and Mary, then knelt before Cardinal Pole, and in a dramatic speech he absolved them.

Two days after that, the King and the Cardinal sat at an open window to hear the Lord Chancellor preach outside St Paul's Cathedral on the text, 'Now we must arouse ourselves from sleep.' The Cardinal had given him the power to grant absolution, and his huge congregation of fifteen hundred people knelt before him in a moving and impressive scene. When Christmas came, there were special rejoicings, and the choristers of both Mary's and Philip's chapels joined together for a particularly splendid service. It was probably for this occasion that Thomas Tallis composed his new and significant Mass, 'Unto us a son is born'.

There was still much to be done, of course. Although the nobles were being allowed to keep Church lands, Mary hoped to set them an example by returning the ecclesiastical property now owned by the Crown. In fact, she was never able to do so because of her own financial difficulties. More straightforward was the pressing need for repairs to churches. Buildings had been neglected, and plate and other furnishings had been taken away by Edward VI's commissioners. There items would have to be sorted out and restored to their proper owners. There were numerous vacancies, too, so priests would have to be trained and appointed and, most urgently of all there was the problem of what to do with the heretics.

Like other Roman Catholic rulers of the day confronting the rise of Protestantism, Mary believed that most of her Protestant subjects had been led astray by a dangerous few, those preachers who were determined to challenge the very existence of the monarchy by spreading subversive, heretical opinions. Such men were the most blameworthy of all, for they used their intelligence and their learning to delude the ignorant. Once they were removed and punished, their misguided followers could be brought back to the proper way of thinking.

The legal mechanism for punishing Protestants now existed, for the recent Parliament had re-enacted the medieval heresy laws. By their provisions, heresy was once more punishable by death, and the goods and property of the guilty would be forfeited to the Crown. The English bishops were eager to put the new legislation into effect, and Mary had no qualms about it. A few months later she was noting in a memorandum for her council that heretics should be punished 'without rashness', justice being done 'to such as by learning would seem to deceive the simple'.

At first the Lord Chancellor thought that he could frighten the leaders of the heretics into fleeing the country, but when various imprisoned preachers were brought before him at his house in Southwark on 22 January 1555, he could see that they were not going to submit. He offered them clemency if they ceased their illegal activities, but they scornfully rejected the suggestion. Six days later, he and several other bishops presided over the trial of John Hooper, recently Bishop of Gloucester, John Rogers, who had been chaplain to the English merchants in Antwerp, and John Cardmaster, a former friar. All three were found guilty and condemned to death.

Rogers was the first to go to the stake, on the morning of 4 February. He died praying for his enemies, while his family and friends wept helplessly and those who had come to watch out of mere curiosity were moved by his

Charter granted by Mary to the Monastery of Westminster, with portraits of herself and Philip, 1556.
(By courtesy of the Dean and Chapter of Westminster)

courage. Laurence Saunders, a former vicar in London, died at the stake in Coventry on 8 February. John Hooper was burned in Gloucester the following day, and Rowland Taylor went to the stake in Suffolk, where he had been rector of a parish. Robert Ferrer, formerly Bishop of St David's was burned on 30 March and John Cardmaster two months later. Thus did the burnings go on, but instead of being intimidated, the Protestants and their sympathisers were inspired by the demeanour of the condemned men, and filled with hatred of the Queen.

In all, 275 men and women went to the stake during Mary's reign. John Foxe listed them in his book, *Acts and Monuments of the English Martyrs*, better known as 'Foxe's Book of Martyrs', and the merciful Mary, who was welcomed by the rejoicing crowds at the time of her accession, became Bloody Mary, persecutor of the innocent. Simon Renard was not the only person to warn the royal couple that the campaign against the heretics was endangering their throne, but the Queen did not listen. For her, there was no dilemma. The heretics who were condemned were evil men, traitors who must be punished, and she could not forgive them. Philip's attitude is not clear. Presumably he approved of the burnings, but his father was still urging him to go slowly in matters of religion and he may have seen the dangers. If he tried to point them out to Mary, his remonstrations had no effect. Eager though she was to please him, she could not compromise her conscience, and the burnings went on.

Realising that they would not solve the problem of heresy in the kingdom, Philip was anxiously considering what might happen when the time came for his wife to give birth to her child. There was a very real possibility that she would die in childbed and, if she did, the Protestants might rebel and put Elizabeth on the throne, killing him in the process. What was to be done? If he and Mary excluded Elizabeth from the succession, the next heir would be Mary, Queen of Scots, the future daughter-in-law of the King of France. She would become Queen of England, and that was an unthinkable prospect.

Philip decided that the only solution was to neutralise Elizabeth by marrying her to some safe, Roman Catholic ally of the Emperor. Emmanuel Philibert, Duke of Savoy, a personable young man and an experienced soldier, would be a suitable candidate. Philip had invited him to spend the previous Christmas in England, but Elizabeth was still at Woodstock, of course, and Mary had refused to let them meet. Philip was therefore proceeding with caution. He could not risk upsetting Mary, but he was determined to get her agreement to the wedding before she was brought to bed.

Tactful conversations with his wife were second nature to Philip now, but although he remained restrained and courteous, he was finding her constant emotional demands wearing in the extreme. Long ago, his father's ambassador Van der Delft, had spoken of how Mary 'clung' to him for support. Her continuing lack of confidence meant that she was constantly seeking reassurance, but could never be satisfied.

Van der Delft, Renard and the others, pitying her, had managed to tolerate her dependence, but they, after all, could always retreat to the privacy of their own residences. There was no such escape for Philip, and whenever he hinted that his father wanted him to go over to the Low Countries, he provoked not only storms of tears from his wife but reproachful reminders from her old ally, Renard.

'Your Highness, is it true, might wish that she was more agreeable,' wrote the ambassador, 'but on the other hand she is infinitely virtuous', 'Your Highness, like a magnanimous Prince, must remember her condition and exert yourself . . . to assist her' and 'Although it might be wished that the Queen were more gracious, your own virtue, goodness and intelligence leave nothing to be desired . . .' In the end, Philip agreed to postpone his departure until his wife had been safely delivered.

On 4 April 1555 the royal couple moved to Hampton Court where, towards the end of the month, the Queen entered the official period of privacy which

The retrochoir of Southwark Cathedral, where the heresy trials were held.
(By courtesy of the Dean and Chapter of Southwark Cathedral: photograph, Jarrold Publishing)

preceded a royal birth. She gave no more public audiences and no one was allowed to enter her apartments except her husband and her ladies. She was supposed to spend forty days in seclusion, but her women were forecasting that she would be delivered before 9 June.

All the leading peers and their ladies flocked to court, guards about the King and Queen were doubled, and at last decisions were taken about Edward Courtenay and Elizabeth. On Philip's urging, Courtenay was released from his prison at Fotheringhay Castle, and allowed to go to the Continent. He was anxious to complete his education by visiting Italy, but he was told that first of all he must travel to the court of Charles V. The Emperor would see that he caused no trouble. The day after his departure, Elizabeth was brought to Hampton Court and was lodged in apartments near Philip's own.

Still in disgrace, she was permitted few visitors and was certainly not invited to see the Queen, but some days after her arrival Mary sent her a fine dress with instructions that she was to wear it that evening. The King was going to pay her a visit. Philip was undoubtedly curious to meet his sister-in-law for himself, and although no record of their encounter has survived, it seems to have gone well. At any rate, Mary finally agreed to receive Elizabeth.

They met late one night in the Queen's apartments, Elizabeth throwing herself on her knees, weeping and vowing that she was innocent of any part in Wyatt's conspiracy. Mary almost believed her; almost, but not entirely. As always, she found her sister unfathomable. There was the apparent truthfulness, the eagerness to please, but there was also that unsettling resemblance to Anne Boleyn and a reserve, a wariness, a concealment of what Elizabeth was really thinking. When they had spoken at length Mary could only shake her head, murmuring, 'Who knows?' According to John Foxe, Philip was present throughout the interview, concealed behind a tapestry. Whether that was so or not, he continued to urge his wife to reinstate her sister, and as a result Elizabeth stayed at court, free to see her friends and members of the Privy Council, while Mary sat on the floor of her bedchamber, her knees drawn up to her chin, waiting for her labour pains to start.

*Elizabeth*, probably painted in the late 1550s, by an unknown artist.
(National Portrait Gallery, London)

# 10

## THE LONELY WIFE

*A*T THE BEGINNING of May 1555, the merchants of Antwerp received a report that a prince had been born to the Queen of England on 30 April. The Queen Dowager ordered the bells to peal and there were excited celebrations, all too soon quenched. The story had been no more than a false report. Slowly the days crept by, the weather grew hotter, nerves became more and more strained and at the end of the month Mary went out into the garden for some fresh air. Philip's friend Ruy Gomez saw her there, stepping out so briskly 'that it seems to me that there is no hope at all for this month'. Amidst the growing scepticism of the courtiers and French speculation that she was suffering from a tumour, the Queen's midwife and her own ladies were insistent that she really was pregnant. Many of them were themselves married women and mothers, and they must have known that something was amiss, but what else could they do but reassure their tearful, anxious and increasingly desperate mistress?

On 1 June, Mary thought that she felt some pains, but they passed off again. Her doctors predicted that she would be delivered on 6 June. When that date came and went they spoke of 24 June, and then 3 July. 'The expressions on people's faces are strange,' wrote Renard, and there were wicked rumours that the Queen was going to pass off someone else's baby as her own. In fact, Mary had been more cruelly deceived than anyone else.

Historians have often assumed that she suffered a phantom pregnancy, the result of her overwhelming desire to bear a child. That may be so. The passage of four centuries and the imprecise nature of contemporary descriptions of her condition make it very difficult to tell. There are other possibilities, however. She may actually have been pregnant at the start. There was a rumour that spring that she had passed a 'lump of flesh'. This would describe the condition medically known as a 'missed abortion', when the fetus had died in the uterus, been partially resorbed and then discharged. Alternatively, conception might have occurred, but with the fetus and the placenta not forming properly. The cells in this situation are very active and form a 'mole'. The French ambassador that spring reported that Mary was suffering from a 'mola'.

Mary was not necessarily deluding herself that she was pregnant, either knowingly or unknowingly. Experiencing as she did all the expected symptoms, it may well be that there really was a fetus, for a short time at least. If so, it is a double cruelty that writers ever since have attributed her claim that she was pregnant to ignorance, wishful thinking, emotional or even mental disturbance, not to say deliberate deceit.

Whatever the real explanation, she was forced to confront the possibility that God was not going to send her a child that summer and that there would be no Roman Catholic heir, no charming baby of her own, no fine son for her adored husband. Philip himself, reserved and fastidious, found the situation more than he could bear. He had to get away, yet how could he manage to detach himself from his pitiful, pathetic wife? For once, his composure deserted him, and he wrote a desperate note to Ruy Gomez, begging him for advice on 'what line I am to take with the Queen about leaving her and about religion. I see I must say something, but God help me!'

Passport prepared for Lord Howard of Effingham to go to Charles V with news of the birth of a son to Mary and Philip, May 1555. Their signatures are at the top.
(Public Record Office, SP69/6/380)

*Philip II, about the time of the Siege of St Quentin*, 1557, by Mor.
(The Escorial, Madrid: photograph authorised by the Patrimonio Nacional)

 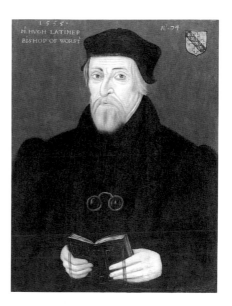

*Nicholas Ridley, Bishop of London*, by an
unknown artist, 1555.
(National Portrait Gallery, London)

*Hugh Latimer, Bishop of Worcester*, by an
unknown artist, 1555.
(National Portrait Gallery, London)

On the following day, 3 August, they all moved briefly to Oatlands from
Hampton Court, to allow it to be cleaned and, as there was much less room at
Oatlands, many of the noblemen and their wives returned to their homes.
Soon afterwards, Mary and Philip went back to Hampton Court. Nothing was
said and no public announcement was made. Gradually Mary, beyond
despair, began to give audiences again and resumed her public life. To the
astonishment of everyone she looked better than she had done for months.
There were no longer any signs of pregnancy and no one dared mention the
subject. When the French ambassador did risk a sly reference to her coming
confinement, she cut him short.

Somehow, Philip managed to break the news of his imminent departure,
and Mary wrote a note to the Emperor. She was grateful to him for allowing
her husband to stay with her until now, she said, but as there was 'nothing in
the world that I set so much store by as the King's presence', she firmly hoped
that his absence would be brief.

On Monday 26 August 1555 they moved to Greenwich, and that Thursday
Philip took his leave of Mary. She had spoken of going with him as far as
Dover, but in the event they parted at the riverside, he assuring her that he
would be back soon. In the meantime, Cardinal Pole had promised to take care
of her. She retained her composure with difficulty, and as soon as the King
had entered the royal barge she hurried into the palace again. The people
below saw her at a window, weeping inconsolably, while Philip waved and
made affectionate gestures to her as his vessel bore him down the river and
finally out of sight.

Writing to him almost every day and trying to ignore the tormenting
rumours that he was diverting himself with the young women of the
Netherlands, Mary made preparations for the next session of Parliament and
awaited the trial of two notable heretics. Nicholas Ridley, former Bishop of
London, and Hugh Latimer, once Bishop of Worcester, had been in prison

Stephen Gardiner's Chantry Chapel in Winchester Cathedral, where Bishop Gardiner was buried. (Royal Commission on the Historical Monuments of England)

since the beginning of her reign. Now they were convicted and their executions were fixed for 16 October in Oxford. 'Be of good comfort, Master Ridley, and play the man!' exclaimed old Latimer as they were chained to the stake. 'We shall this day light such a candle by God's grace in England as I trust shall never be put out.' With their deaths, public sympathy for the martyrs and hatred of Mary reached new heights.

Five days later, she opened Parliament. Its elected members were unruly and resentful, and her Lord Chancellor mortally ill. The Bishop of Winchester was suffering from what must have been prostate trouble, and he was so weak that it took four men to support him as his horse paced along slowly to Westminster. The Queen needed revenues, and with one final, tremendous effort, the Chancellor made his speech asking the members to vote her supplies. He was so exhausted afterwards that he could not return to his own residence and Mary lodged him in her palace. There he lay, receiving visits from friends and enemies alike. Lord Paget and he were finally reconciled, just before he died.

Parliament did vote the Queen the subsidy she needed, but she dared not ask their approval for her plan to have Philip crowned King of England and, when a measure was introduced to summon and forfeit all who had left the realm without permission, such an uproar broke out that she dissolved Parliament and sent the leaders of the opposition to the Tower.

She spent Christmas 1555 at Greenwich, in an atmosphere of gloom. Early in January, she appointed Nicholas Heath, the Archbishop of York, to succeed

Stephen Gardiner as Chancellor. Lord Paget, who had wanted the post himself, was deeply disappointed, and the divisions within the Privy Council grew worse than ever. A plot by Henry Dudley to depose Mary in favour of Elizabeth was discovered in March 1556, leaving the Queen feeling even more desperate to see her husband again.

Hopefully, she instructed her envoy in the Low Countries to ask the King if she should keep ready the fleet which would escort him when he sailed back to England. He was not only to tell Philip that she needed the comfort of her presence, he was also to point out that they could yet have children. Back came vague promises, but no sign of Philip himself. She therefore wrote the Emperor a pathetic letter begging him to let her husband return, and she dispatched Lord Paget to Philip himself, with letters and a gift of rings. Trying to be kind, Paget made Philip's formal enquiries about her health sound more personal than they probably were. Charles V had not yet resigned the Empire to his brother, nor had he yet left for the monastery in Spain where he planned to end his days. Despite his ill-health, he was still keenly interested in English affairs. How was the Queen, he had enquired, to which Lord Paget replied that she 'did indifferently well, as one might do that wanted of that you loved above all earthly things'. Philip had hastily intervened to say that he would be back in England in a few weeks' time, without a doubt.

On 21 March 1556, Thomas Cranmer was sent to the stake. In his final weeks, Henry VIII's Archbishop of Canterbury signed a series of statements renouncing his Protestant beliefs, but even then Mary refused to pardon him. He had been the friend of Anne Boleyn, the man who had made possible her mother's divorce. There could be no forgiveness for him. He was burned at Oxford, thrusting his right hand into the flames first, because with it he had signed his recantations. By now, most people were sickened by these constant spectacles of death and the Protestants were eagerly awaiting the day when Mary would be dead and Elizabeth would sit on her throne instead.

Mary scarcely cared about reports of unrest. 'I cannot but deeply feel the solitude in which the King's absence leaves me,' she wrote to Charles V. 'As your Majesty well knows, he is the chief joy and comfort I have in the world.'

The Burning of Archbishop Cranmer, an illustration to Acts and Monuments of the English Martyrs, by John Foxe. (National Portrait Gallery, London)

*The Abdication of Charles V*, by Frans Francken. Philip is on the right, his uncle Ferdinand on the left.
(Rijksmuseum, Amsterdam)

The Emperor replied that his son hoped to be in England before the end of June but, of course, an impending visit to Brussels by the King and Queen of Bohemia might delay him. Possessed by a new bitterness, Mary wept, inveighed against her faithless counsellors and could sleep for no more than two or three hours each night. The French ambassador noted gloatingly that she had aged ten years in the last few months, and Mrs Clarentius was heard to wish that the marriage had never taken place.

'My Lord,' wrote Mary to the Emperor on 15 July, 'now that June is over and July drawing to an end, it would be pleasanter for me to be able to thank your Majesty for sending me back the King my lord and good husband ... however, as your Majesty has been pleased to break your promise in this connection, a promise you made to me regarding the return of the King my husband, I must perforce be satisfied, although to my unspeakable regret.' She had never before used that tone to her old friend and protector, and there were even tales that she had angrily slashed a portrait of Philip which hung in her apartments.

Rage as she might, he still did not come, and her mood of anger passed. By early September she had reverted to her accustomed humble pleading, imploring Charles 'to consider the miserable plight into which this country has now fallen' without Philip to see to affairs of state. She was not, she alleged, 'moved by my personal desire for his presence, although I do unspeakably long to have him here', but for the good of the kingdom she begged him to send her husband back.

This time, her pleas seemed to have some effect. Suddenly, members of

140

Philip's retinue began returning to London, there were regular messages from him, and she began to hope that he really was preparing to come to England again. That same month brought reassuring news from Venice. Finally allowed by Charles V to travel to Italy, Edward Courtenay had caught a violent fever and died. At least no one would plot on his behalf again. But there remained the problem of Elizabeth. Philip still wanted to marry her to the Duke of Savoy, and he was being very insistent. Mary was against the idea, but if it would please her husband she would withdraw her objections.

On 28 November 1556 Elizabeth rode back to court with an impressive retinue of over two hundred gentlemen. It was said that she came at her own urgent request, and a stormy audience with the Queen ensued. Mary insisted that she accept the Duke, Elizabeth refused and Mary threatened her with the Tower. In a panic, the younger woman thought of fleeing to France, but the fear that by so doing she would forfeit any chance of inheriting the throne prevented her. Instead, she had a long interview with Cardinal Pole, whom she had never before met, and then she rode back to Hatfield again.

Spending Christmas at Greenwich as usual, the Queen was in a mood of excited anticipation. Developments on the Continent made it virtually certain that Philip would soon be with her. The recently elected Pope, Paul IV, was from Naples, and he had persuaded the French to join him in an attempt to drive the Habsburg forces out of Italy. Philip had decided to create a diversion in the north by invading France, and he wanted English assistance. If he was to persuade the Queen and her Privy Council to agree, he would have to do so in person.

Sure enough, on 18 March 1557, he arrived at Dover, travelled to Gravesend and sailed up the Thames. Mary and he were reunited at Greenwich, and the following day bells pealed out over London and a *Te Deum* was sung in every church. The King and Queen rode in state to Westminster together, and a few days later they received some distinguished visitors there. Philip's cousin the Duchess of Lorraine, his half-sister the Duchess of Parma and her twelve-year-old son had come over, ostensibly to help persuade Elizabeth to marry the Duke of Savoy and perhaps to lend the King himself some moral support in his dealing with his wife. Philip greeted them at the waterside and took them upstairs to meet Mary. They all spent Easter together at Greenwich, and when they were back in London the Queen gave a lavish farewell banquet for the visitors.

There are no eye-witness descriptions this time of lengthy conversations between the King and Queen but, for all Mary's past hurt and resentment, they soon seem to have fallen into their former pleasant relationship, he courteous and respectful, she happy at last. Both knew that his stay would be brief, and Mary lost no time in seeing her Privy Councillors, one by one, in an attempt to persuade them to allow England to enter the war as Philip's ally.

The Scots would be sure to support the French, and added reason to take action came in April when Thomas Stafford, an obstreperous nephew of Cardinal Pole, suddenly sailed from France, where he had been living in exile, to the Yorkshire coast. With two French ships, he managed to seize the half-ruined Scarborough Castle. He was arrested a few days later, but in spite of Henry II's vigorous denials, the English were convinced that he had initiated the raid. On 1 May, England declared war on France.

Furious at his enemies, the Habsburgs, the Pope was recalling the legates he had appointed to Philip's dominions, and he sent for Cardinal Pole. The

Cardinal was to go at once to Rome, under suspicion of heresy. Mary was horrified when she heard the news. She refused to let him risk his life by going, and she was even more insulted when Paul IV announced that he was appointing William Peto as his legate to England instead. Peto had once been her confessor, it was true, but he was an aged friar with no other claim to fame. To appoint such a nonentity was a downright insult, and her attitude towards the papacy underwent an immediate change. She no longer felt any qualms about supporting her husband's hostility towards Paul IV.

The thought that she could make a real contribution to Philip's new enterprise evidently consoled her to some extent for his departure. They left London together, and at three in the morning on 6 July they said their farewells in Dover, at the water's edge. Philip had a quick crossing and he was soon in Brussels, preparing to lead his army. A contingent of English soldiers led by the Earl of Pembroke joined his forces, and on 27 August 1557 the King's army gained a notable victory, when they took the town of St Quentin by storm. More *Te Deums* were sung in London, and Philip went on to capture various other fortresses in the neighbourhood. By the end of October, his army was taking up its winter quarters, and most of the English returned triumphantly home.

Henry II was not about to let this public humiliation go unavenged, and at the end of the year he made his move. Ever since 1347 the English had held Calais, an invaluable foothold on French soil. Now the French army besieged the town, and they captured it early in January 1558. This was a bitter blow. The English were furious, blaming Philip and his army for not coming to their assistance in time. The Spaniards, for their part, said that the English should

*William Herbert, 1st Earl of Pembroke*, by an unknown artist, 1557.
(The Hamilton Collection)

have held out longer and, to add insult to injury, Philip allowed his Flemish merchants to provide supplies for the French garrison now in position in the town.

John Foxe alleged that Mary, when she heard, exclaimed that on her death the word 'Calais' would be found written on her heart. Cardinal Pole told Philip that she received the news in a spirit of patient acceptance, and in that same letter he imparted a startling piece of news. The Queen, he said, was sure that she was pregnant again.

When he had recovered from the shock, Philip composed a reply which was a masterpiece of kindly tact. No doubt he knew full well that Mary would be waiting tremulously to see his answer. He thanked the Cardinal for the news 'of the pregnancy of the Queen, my beloved wife, which has given me greater joy than I can express to you, as it is the one thing in the world I have most desired and which is of the greatest importance for the cause of religion and the welfare of the realm. I therefore render thanks to Our Lord for this great mercy he has shown us, and I am obliged to you for the news you have given me of it, which has gone far to lighten the sorrow I have felt for the loss of Calais.'

Anxious to persuade the English to raise more men and retake the town, he sent his friend the Count de Feria to London with messages for the Queen. Mary would rather have had Philip himself, but she understood that he could not come, and the Count was kind and comforting. He had fallen in love with her favourite lady-in-waiting, Jane Dormer, and Jane no doubt enlisted his sympathy for her mistress. Moreover, the Count could see for himself that if anything were to be done for Philip, it would be achieved by the Queen and not by her councillors. 'It would be well if all those who govern this kingdom shared the Queen's spirit,' he told Philip after his first audience.

Her council was as divided as ever, and a month later he was complaining, 'I am at my wits' end with these people here, as God shall be my witness, and do not know what to do. Your Majesty must realise that from night to morning and morning to night they change everything they have decided, and it is impossible to make them see what a state they are in. The Queen tells me she is doing all she can. It is true she has spirit and good will. With the rest, it is hard labour.' Mary managed to get Parliament to vote her a generous sum in supplies. Ailing though she was, the Venetian ambassador had recently been much impressed by her intellect as well as by her piercing grey eyes.

She was saying little about her pregnancy, but towards the end of February 1558 she entered into the traditional seclusion preceding her confinement, which she believed would be in March. The Count had grave doubts, however. 'The one thing that matters to her is that your Majesty come hither,' he told Philip, 'and it seems to me she is making herself believe that she is with child, although she does not own up to it.'

On 30 March she made her will. She was forty-two years old. 'Thinking myself to be with child in lawful marriage between my said dearly beloved husband and lord,' it began, 'I be at this present (thanks be unto Almighty God) otherwise in good health, yet foreseeing the great danger which by God's ordinance remains to all women in their travail of children, have thought good both for discharge of my conscience and continuance of good order within my realm and dominions to declare my last will and testament.' Her husband would be her chief executor, and the document is full of loving references to him.

By the end of April she had to resign herself to the fact that, once more, she was mistaken. The false symptoms of pregnancy began to fade, leaving her weak, ill and unable to sleep. Wretchedly aware of having failed her husband again, she lived in terror of offending him. When the King of Sweden sent an envoy to ask for Elizabeth's hand for his son, she was reminded that she had not yet managed to persuade her sister to marry the Duke of Savoy. Philip was urging the match yet again, and she wrote him an urgent little note. 'I beseech you in all humility,' she begged, 'to put off the business until your return . . . for otherwise your Highness will be angry against me, and that will be worse than death for me, for I have already begun to taste your anger all too often, to my great sorrow.'

She hoped that he might come in May, but he did not. 'I had greatly desired to go,' Philip wrote to Feria, 'and it would have given the Queen and myself much happiness had I been able to do so . . . I thank you for keeping the Queen company and the devotion you show in her service, and affectionately beg you so to continue, to cheer her loneliness, for thus you are doing us the greatest pleasure.' She received the news more quietly than the Count expected, but she scarcely seemed to grasp the message, for she gave orders that the fleet which would escort the King should wait in readiness at Dunkirk and Dover, and that lodgings between London and the coast should be prepared for him.

The Greenwich armour of William, 1st Earl of Pembroke and his horse, about 1550.
(Glasgow Museums: Art Gallery & Museum, Kelvingrove)

*Lady Jane Dormer*, Mary's favourite lady-in-waiting, later Duchess of
Feria, by Mor, about 1560.

The Count went back to the Low Countries a few weeks later, and at the end
of the summer Mary had a bout of fever, something new for her. It has often
been said that by now she was suffering from cancer, probably from an
ovarian tumour, but her symptoms make this unlikely. The latest medical
opinion suggests that she had contracted either tuberculosis (which seems to
have killed both her half-brothers Edward and the Duke of Richmond),
influenza or some other generalised infection. Soon she was wracked by
violent paroxysms of an unspecified nature. These would fit in with this
diagnosis and would presumably have been either high fevers or even
epileptic seizures.

Becoming progressively weaker, she had a lucid interval on 28 October 1558
and made a codicil to her will. 'Forasmuch as God hath hitherto sent me no
fruit nor heir of my body,' and, 'feeling myself presently sick and weak in
body and yet of whole and perfect remembrance, Our Lord be thanked', she
thought it best to add a few paragraphs to her former will. If she did indeed
die childless, she asked her lawful successor to allow her executors to carry out
the provisions of that will. Although, 'my said most Dear Lord and Husband

shall for default of heir of my body have no further government, order and rule within this realm and the dominions belonging thereto', she asked him to remain the father, brother and friend of England and its next monarch. She did not, however, say who that monarch should be.

Her councillors had been pressing her constantly to recognise Elizabeth as her heir. For months she had refused. Even when Philip had sent her his confessor the previous year to urge her to do so, she had angrily retorted that Elizabeth was no sister of hers. She declared that the infamous Anne Boleyn had taken lovers, and she said it was well known that Anne's daughter was the child of Mark Smeaton, her lute player. Now, however, with the end so near, the painful jealousy and fear seemed to ebb away. She agreed at last that Elizabeth should have her crown, asking only that the new Queen should maintain the old religion as she herself had restored it, be kind to her servants and pay her debts. That done, she lapsed into unconsciousness again.

Philip knew by now that she was gravely ill, but he was distracted by other events. Word had just reached him that Charles V had died in his monastery in Spain and he had hardly recovered from the initial shock, when another messenger arrived to tell him that his aunt, the Queen Dowager, had died too. 'You may imagine what a state I am in,' he wrote to his sister, Joanna. 'It seems to me that everything is being taken from me at once . . . The Queen my wife has been ill and although she has recovered somewhat her infirmities are such that grave fears must be entertained on her score.' He had retired to a monastery on hearing of his father's death, and he could not possibly leave the country before the Emperor's memorial service. Instead, he sent the Count de Feria back to England, with one of his own physicians.

By the time the Count arrived in London, Mary was far gone. The infection had probably spread to cause meningitis, for she had been drifting in and out of consciousness for some days past, telling her ladies dreamily that she was

*Nicholas Heath, Archbishop of York* and Mary's second Lord Chancellor, by Eworth, 1566.
(National Portrait Gallery, London)

*Cesare Adelmare of Genoa*, one of Mary's doctors, 1558, attributed to Flicke.
(C Cottrell-Dormer, Rousham: photograph, Courtauld Institute of Art)

seeing many little children like angels playing before her, singing pleasing notes. On 16 November 1558, Lord Chancellor Heath and her Privy Councillors went into her chamber to perform a solemn ceremony. In keeping with custom, they had to read out her will.

The Queen had lapsed into unconsciousness again, and she did not know that they were there. Next morning, when Mass was celebrated in her chamber, she roused herself. For the last time she made her responses, clearly and distinctly. She lay quietly after that, watching the priest take the sacred elements, and then she closed her eyes and died. Many years later, married to the Count de Feria and living in Spain, Jane Dormer described her mistress's last moments to a friend, and the tears poured down her cheeks.

Cardinal Pole had been unable to comfort Mary in her final illness, for all that autumn he had himself been suffering from a recurrent fever. His servants tried to keep the news of Mary's death from him, but he could see from their faces that something was amiss, and they had to tell him. He died that same evening.

While the Privy Councillors rode down to Hatfield to let Elizabeth know that she was Queen, Viscount Montague set out for the Low Countries to inform Philip. 'May God have received her in his glory,' the King wrote in a postscript to his letter to his sister. An excess of grief was never allowable to the true believer but, using the words he always did to describe his reaction to the loss of a close relative, he went on, 'I felt a reasonable regret for her death,' and he added, 'I shall miss her . . .'

In her will she had left him, 'to keep for a memory of me', the diamond Charles V had sent her on her betrothal, the diamond Philip had given the Marquis de Las Navas for her, a gold collar set with nine diamonds which he had presented to her on the first Epiphany after their wedding, and another of his gifts, a ruby ring sent to her with the Count de Feria. She had made numerous other bequests to convents and monasteries, councillors, servants and friends.

Philip did not receive the jewels, nor were her other instructions carried out, but Elizabeth did accord her a funeral befitting a Queen. Mary's body was opened and embalmed by her surgeons and physicians. Her heart was placed in a silver and purple velvet box, and buried in the Chapel Royal in St James's Palace. Her lead coffin was draped with purple velvet and lace, and placed in her black-hung Privy Chamber on two trestle tables covered in cloth of gold. There she lay in state, watched over by her praying ladies.

On 10 December 1558, a long procession of dignitaries formed and the coffin was carried beneath a purple velvet canopy, fringed with gold and blue, to the Chapel Royal in the palace. The entire chapel had been hung with black and decorated with the Queen's coat of arms. In the centre stood a magnificent catafalque, surrounded by four circles of huge candles. Wax figures of mourning angels and queens in their robes decorated the sides of the bier and beneath it was a great dome painted in gold, with representations of the four evangelists.

Lords and ladies, a herald and a pursuivant, servants and priests guarded their mistress's body day and night, while her bishops and choristers sang the Dirge, the Mass of Our Lady, the Mass of the Holy Ghost and the Requiem Mass. Finally, on 14 December, before a silent crowd, the coffin was carried out to an elaborate black chariot. A rich pall was placed over it, and on top of that was laid the presentation, a life-sized, painted effigy of the Queen

The Chapel Royal,
St James's Palace,
where Mary lay in
state.
(HM Chapel Royal,
St James's Palace ©
Her Majesty The Queen)

Head of the effigy of Mary made for
her funeral.
(By courtesy of the Dean and Chapter
of Westminster)

The effigy, by her serjeant painter,
Nicholas Lizard, cost £6. 13s. 4d.
(By courtesy of the Dean and Chapter
of Westminster)

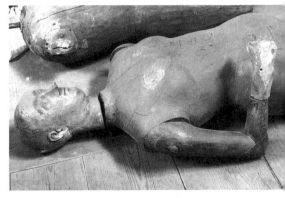

*Opposite.* Monument to Elizabeth I in
Westminster Abbey, with plaque on the
right commemorating Mary I.
(By courtesy of the Dean and Chapter of
Westminster: photograph, A F Kersting)

wearing her crown and her royal robes. The long procession rode through the streets to Westminster Abbey, where Mary was buried in Henry VII's chapel.

She had asked in her will that her mother's body should be brought from Peterborough to rest beside her own, and that monuments should be set up over them, 'for a decent memory to us'. Nothing was done, and Catherine of Aragon's remains are still in Peterborough Cathedral. Queen Elizabeth had no desire to encourage Roman Catholic sentiments in once more Protestant England. When she herself died in 1603, she was laid in the same vault as her sister, and it was left to King James VI and I to put up an elaborate memorial to his predecessors. It has pillars, coats of arms and sculptured lions guarding an effigy of Elizabeth, and a flattering eulogy of her. Near the base, beneath one of the lions, another small plaque notes in Latin that Mary lies there too, 'in hope of the Resurrection'.

# FURTHER READING

*THE PRINCIPAL* sources for the life of Mary I are the various Calendars of State Papers, notably the *Calendar of State Papers: Spanish*, edited by R Tyler and others (1862–1954), the *Calendar of State Papers (Domestic Series) 1547–80*, edited by R Lemon and others, and the *Calendar of State Papers: Venetian*, edited by R Brown and others (1844–98). For Mary's childhood, Garrett Mattingly, *Catherine of Aragon* (Boston 1941), J J Scarisbrick, *Henry VIII* (1968), D Starkey, *The Reign of Henry VIII* (1991) and E W Ives, *Anne Boleyn* (Oxford 1986) provide very readable accounts of the political events of the time. F Madden, *Privy Purse Expenses of the Princess Mary* (1831) has fascinating evidence of her expenditure, and Sydney Anglo's 'La Salle de Banquet et le Théatre construits à Greenwich pour les Fêtes Franco-Anglaises de 1527', in *Le Lieu Théâtral à la Renaissance* (Paris 1964), recreates Mary's betrothal to the Duke of Orleans.

*The Chronicle of Queen Jane and of Two Years of Queen Mary*, edited by J G Nicholas (Camden Society 1850), is a contemporary account of the events after the death of Edward VI, and David Matthew, *Lady Jane Grey: The Setting of the Reign* (1972) is a touching biography. Mary's flight to East Anglia is described in Robert Wingfield, 'Vitae Mariae Reginae', edited by D MacCulloch (*Camden Miscellany* xxviii, 1984). Professor David Loades has analysed Mary's reign in admirable detail in his scholarly publications, particularly *The Reign of Mary Tudor* (1979, 1991) and *Mary Tudor, A Life* (Oxford 1989).

Cardinal Pole found a biographer in W Schenk, *Reginald Pole, Cardinal of England* (1950), while Glyn Redworth, *In Defence of the Church Catholic: The Life of Stephen Gardiner*, studies Mary's first Lord Chancellor, whose correspondence is to be found in J A Muller, *The Letters of Stephen Gardiner* (Cambridge 1933). 'Foxe's Book of Martyrs' is more properly John Foxe, *Acts and Monuments of the English Martyrs* and is published in many editions, for example S R Cattley (1837–41). Renard and Noailles are the principal protagonists in E Harris Harbison, *Rival Ambassadors at the Court of Queen Mary* (Princeton 1940), the correspondence of the French ambassadors being printed in René de Vertot, *Ambassades de MM de Noailles en Angleterre* (1763).

Popular biographies of Philip II include Edward Grierson, *King of Two Worlds: Philip of Spain* (1974) and Geoffrey Parker, *Philip II* (1979). Mary's costume is intelligently analysed by Alison J Carter, 'Mary Tudor's Wardrobe' in *Costume: The Journal of the Costume Society* xviii (1984). The story of her favourite lady-in-waiting is told in H Clifford, *The Life of Jane Dormer, Duchess of Feria*, edited by J Stevenson (1882), and Mary's relationship with Elizabeth is further explored in Rosalind K Marshall, *Elizabeth I* (HMSO 1991).